The Future Is Fluid Form

Practical Steps for Designing Flat, Flexible Organizations

Ord Elliott

iUniverse, Inc.

New York   Bloomington

iUniverse books may be ordered through booksellers or by contacting:

iUniverse
1663 Liberty Drive
Bloomington, IN 47403
www.iuniverse.com
1-800-Authors (1-800-288-4677)

ISBN: 978-1-4401-1537-0 (pbk)
ISBN: 978-1-4401-1539-4 (dj)
ISBN: 978-1-4401-1538-7 (ebk)

Library of Congress Control Number: 2008912103

Printed in the United States of America

iUniverse rev. date: 01/22/2009

Has your enterprise tried everything from Total Quality Management to Process Reengineering and Six Sigma, only to remain chained by functional silos and command-and-control hierarchy? Are you ready to put frustration and bureaucracy in the rearview mirror? In *The Future is Fluid Form*, author Ord Elliott discusses eight steps to building a more effective organization that breaks through the bureaucracy.

The fluid form organizational method relies on having the right people in the right place at the right time. It unlocks productivity, freedom, and high performance by removing the anchors that keep your enterprise from maximizing its investment in people and technology. It:

- Creates robust cross-functional teams and reduces silos
- Flattens organizations
- Gets more accomplished by fewer people in less time
- Provides more flexibility in an enterprise

From Procter and Gamble, General Electric, Allied Signal, Shell Oil, and Pacific Gas and Electric, to the high-tech world of Intel, Philips, Cisco Systems, and Silicon Valley start-ups, Ord has deployed most of the well-known methodologies. He has seen what works and what doesn't. Immersed with real-life examples from world-renowned companies, *The Future is Fluid Form* demonstrates a new way to organize your people, your business, and your future.

For my daughter, Emily

Contents

Preface

In 1980, I was researching the progress and future possibilities of the innovative and very successful manufacturing plants within Procter and Gamble. While these organizations eliminated the need for one or two levels of management by building autonomous and multi-skilled work teams, the management structure above them remained largely the same. The opportunity to extend these concepts into management, I concluded, would create a more fluid form of collaborative leadership along with much greater organization flexibility. In the decades since then I have been part of and seen many companies evolve in this direction. Today Cisco Systems is successfully evolving in this direction, supported by their cutting edge networking and communication technologies. In this book I share a number of these innovations that illustrate how to design what I call *Fluid Form* organization.

Most of my insights have come from experience inside organizations working with clients and other consultants. For fifteen years my longtime friend and consulting colleague, Roland Cavanagh, and I have discussed how to build more effective organizations that really break through the bureaucracy to "get the job done." In many ways this book is the outcome of our consulting time together.

I owe similar thanks to Peg Maddocks who helped me create a different approach to strategic planning when I was starting my consulting business. Her insights on several drafts of this book have proved invaluable as well.

My gratitude and appreciation also go to:

Rosalie Pryor Escamilla for always being there for me when I need to test ideas, whether they be consulting or writing.

Bruce Gates for providing unique and creative insights from his innovative, academic perspective in decision support and operations management.

Lauren Oliver for her support and understanding of how organization design affects gender balance, enabling us all to work together and share leadership.

Bill Trotter for his perspective of the current challenges faced by internal management consultants.

Keith Lawrence for our multi-year updates at the forefront of organization design.

Larry Heasley for the perspective of an executive who is always in the midst of major change.

Ron Ricci for detailing Cisco Sytems' transformation to speed and scale.

Dodd Starbird for insights on how best to present the data to executives.

Mike Vescuso and Eddie Molloy for their practical consultant viewpoint.

Al Chandler, Tom Cummings, and Barry Posner for an academic and historical perspective on the initial concept.

Len Schlesinger who knows change from the academic and business perspective.

Ron Goerss for his experience in executive recruiting and his always enthusiastic and practical approach to management.

Tom Hanks who brought me the history of the Comanche.

Wayne Oler and John Eggen for introducing me to the world of publishing.

Laura Lawson for a publisher's view and advice on early drafts.

Mark Morton for his contribution on writing style.

Michael Levin for significant help in restructuring the book.

Jan Venturini for her intuition and inspiration.

Cutty Smith and my daughter, Emily, for their loving support and encouragement.

Overview

The Future Is Fluid Form

During the eighteenth century the Comanche—a Native American tribe of exceptional warriors and horsemen—became a dominant and powerful force in the Southern Plains. In terms of political and social organization, the Comanche did not operate within a hierarchical structure of command and control like most other tribes. Instead, they worked together assuming fluid roles in order to operate most efficiently. While individuals selected chiefs to guide them, no individual was obliged to accept tribal decisions. An individual merely adapted to his or her necessary role. As one historian wrote:

They selected leaders for war, though the authority of the war chief never extended beyond the war trail. Here the man rarely sought the office; the office sought the man, usually some intelligent, experienced, or lucky warrior ... Hunter warriors cooperated like a pack of wolves, running behind a crafty leader. But failure, or even pure bad luck, quickly destroyed any war chief's prestige and authority, and war leaders rose and fell continually ... Each band had its own civil chief, almost always a powerful family head who had exhibited courage and wisdom in the hunt and in war ... again, the office found the man.[1]

That was their culture. Consequently, the Comanche evolved into one of the most fierce and competitive tribes in North America, completely dominating the Texas plains.

---

1 From *Comanches: The Destruction of a People* by T. R. Fehrenbach, copyright © 1974 Used by permission of Alfred A. Knopf, a division of Random House, Inc.

The successful philosophy that the Comanche utilized is a concept that is integral to revamping your business or organization—it is a concept that I call Fluid Form.

I want to show you how to guide your organization to be as fluid as the Comanche. I will teach you how to be a warrior, how to break out of command-and-control thinking, and how to dominate your marketplace like the Comanche ruled the plains.

How do you get the most out of your organization? How do you maximize productivity with the employees you have? How do you improve performance, effectiveness, and results?

The old approach—hierarchical command-and-control—doesn't work any longer. For two decades, consultants have sought to create change in organizations through building cross-functional projects and processes under banners such as TQM, Process Re-engineering, and Six Sigma. It's not that these approaches fail to garner results. It's just that they aren't successful enough.

The "old school" approach to cross-functionality symbolized by these methods often creates more turmoil than success. They don't get the results people are looking for. People are disappointed in these approaches, and they don't participate. Or they participate at different levels, so that an organization doesn't get a critical mass of focus required in order to achieve the desired result.

Ultimately, if you're a manager, the bottom line is your own success as it reflects the company's success. When you're in charge of an operation, an organization, or a unit—or even if you're a consultant trying to help them improve—if the organization doesn't produce great results, then you aren't successful, either. In a competitive environment like this, companies cannot simply struggle along at a survival level. Instead, they don't survive. The competition defeats them. Why? Because they didn't get the product out in time. They missed the market window. They weren't able to get the sustained commitment from all relevant parties in order to streamline processes and keep the organization competitive.

So how do you create an organization that is less bureaucratic, that gets more work done in a productive manner—that gets the results you want?

The answer is Fluid Form.

To describe Fluid Form most simply, it's *the right people in the right place at the right time.* The key benefits of Fluid Form are as follows:

1. Creates robust cross-functional teams and reduces silos;
2. Flattens organizations;
3. Gets more accomplished by fewer people in less time; and
4. Provides more flexibility in an enterprise.

Fluid form is itself fluid; it can be interpreted and implemented uniquely. What you'll find in this book is not a rigid system that must be followed exactly as described. Instead, it's an approach that is as flexible as the organizations it transforms.

What does that mean, in practical terms? It means you have better problem-solving and decision-making. Problems get solved faster, and organizations make better choices. You can manage complex projects far more successfully. You can reduce project cycle times and the cost of these projects by getting them done efficiently.

You'll be able to react more quickly and effectively as events change in the business environment. As situations change, your organization will be more capable of reformulating itself around the issues of people, projects, and processes essential to achieve results. Fluid Form means reformulating, changing, starting anew, and moving forward. Fluid Form is about optimizing your business.

Bureaucratic organizations waste unused talents, skills, or brainpower (which can atrophy, if not challenged) because people are boxed into a job instead of having multiple and varying opportunities to "show their stuff." Organizations that are fast-paced and require flexibility are best suited for Fluid Form. A Fluid Form organization is better equipped to get the maximum effectiveness out of employee talent, allowing more people different work options because they're not in a bureaucratic structure. This affords them more opportunity, which improves employee work satisfaction.

Fluid Form aligns closely with what Gen-X and Gen-Y employees want in an organization today: more flexibility, more personal development, more growth, and more opportunity to work on different kinds of things. Your younger employees will not be content to be stuck in a "one-job cubbyhole" with a list of required tasks they have to do over and over again. With Fluid Form, they'll be happier, and it will be easier for you to groom them for leadership positions down the road. As individual employees are invited to thrive, the business, as a synergetic entity, is better able to thrive.

Fluid Form is also better at finding the leadership potential in the organization, not just through individual leaders, but through the capabilities of the whole array of talents that your people can bring to bear. It allows for multiple leaders on a project, instead of just one individual running a specific project or situation. Those are the benefits of Fluid Form within the organization.

In a marketplace, Fluid Form enterprises are better at dealing with suppliers' and customers' organizations, because there are more people with the capability to step up and solve problems, to get results, and to find win-win solutions. As a result, your organization develops a more commanding presence in the marketplace, because you display unique flexibility, which makes your competitors appear even more hide-bound by comparison.

As you build Fluid Form, you can reformulate the organization to meet changing business situations; you essentially build change directly into the organization. Once you build in Fluid Form, change becomes the norm within your organization. This solves the problem of resistance to change that occurs every time leaders seek to make shifts. It's a natural human tendency to resist change—until change itself becomes part of the culture. Indeed, with Fluid Form, change *is* the culture. People are being rewarded for playing multiple roles and taking on different jobs. Thus, under Fluid Form, change is how you do business.

It's not just private sector businesses that can benefit from Fluid Form. As we'll see toward the end of the book, many of the big global issues today—health care and education, to name two—could more easily be solved by Fluid Form organizations than by anything that's out there today. It's all about connecting with others in problem-solving, and thus getting real results and getting things done. In what I would call an inter-organizational world, Fluid Form is a much more effective way to move the ball forward.

Can traditional hierarchical organizations learn to become fluid form organizations?

Absolutely. In this book, I will share with you the essentials of Fluid Form, and I will show you how to install it, based on my nearly four decades of experience as a consultant to many of the nation's most respected companies, including Procter & Gamble, Philips, General Electric, Intel, Pacific Gas & Electric, and Shell. The case history involving Procter & Gamble shows where I learned many of the lessons that evolved into Fluid Form. You'll find that story in Step 1.

I'll show you organizations that were able to rid themselves of a hierarchical structure and put Fluid Form into place, and I'll show you the results they achieved. To provide a cautionary aspect to the story, I'll also take you into organizations that, for various reasons, were either unable or unwilling to make the jump to Fluid Form, and I'll show you where they ended up.

Since the advent of TQM, Process Re-engineering, and Six Sigma in the last two decades, there has been virtually no new learning on how to create cross-functional teams and groups. Businesses and organizations have lacked information or education on how to create processes across the various silos to get the right people working together to solve problems in a way that would make a difference. A lot of companies have invested extensively in expensive consulting firms to put cross-functional business processes into place. But as I said at the outset, the results have often been less than satisfactory. What initially works well frequently breaks apart over time, as people find it difficult to stay committed to the process in order to see it through.

At the same time, senior management has to ensure that commitment to breaking down functional and departmental silos and building cross-functional mastery is not simply viewed in the organization as the latest management fad, a "flavor of the month" kind of thing. Unless senior management builds cross-functionality as the bedrock of the organization, it becomes one more thing that simply gets in the way of the "real" work. In Fluid Form, by contrast, cross-functionality is embedded with such robustness that it *is* the real work. Fluid Form is the cutting edge methodology that delivers on the promise of TQM, Process Re-engineering, and Six Sigma. The tools used in these methods actually will be far more successful in a Fluid Form organization.

In a business environment where cost savings and the ability to make nimble moves in the marketplace are vital, and where organizations must flatten to survive, Fluid Form is indeed the answer.

So what is Fluid Form and how is it different from what's out there now?

People talk about organizations that are process and project oriented, or horizontal; but Fluid Form truly is more process and project oriented. It has a bigger bias toward cross-functionality, because there are far fewer functions and vertical stovepipes in Fluid Form.

Coordination and decision-making usually are performed by networks of key stakeholders, instead of issues being resolved up the hierarchy in a traditional command-and-control way. Fluid Form puts an end to "I've got to check with my boss, and you've got to check with your boss, and your boss's boss." It dispenses the traditional approach that requires functional heads or department heads to get together and make decisions. Instead, decisions are made by the key people networks who have a stake in the outcome of a process, who have expertise in how it should run, who understand what the results should be, and who know from experience when these things should get done. As a result, Fluid Form organizations are flatter. There are fewer levels of hierarchy.

In a perfect world, you build a project and process organization with what you have, simply by putting the right people together, regardless of what function they're in. This means you have to examine your staff and place them accordingly. It doesn't mean that your people have to be in their Fluid Form roles all the time. But the earlier they become engaged in a process because they know they are a part of it, the fewer boundaries will have to be managed. You have people working together on key tasks that need to get done. It's a completely different mindset from the hierarchical view, which is where "my department does our thing and your department does your thing and we never meet in the middle." It's the teams that make this whole process work. Once you build the networks the Fluid Form way, you can flatten the organization, because it is network-based.

Cisco Systems is an example of an organization that is seeking to move to a Fluid Form-type approach. They are trying to encourage executives to work more broadly and more collaboratively across the organization.

Chairman and CEO, John Chambers, envisions that the office of the CEO will be less hierarchical in five years—a more collaborative executive suite. "There will probably be a title of CEO, but the next CEO will be more a leader of a council. 'Command and control' is very effective when you're in a couple of product areas or one or two major cross-functional initiatives per year. It is not an effective leadership style or organization structure if you're moving into a lot of market adjacencies and you have a lot of major cross-functional priorities." [2]

The functional, hierarchical organization may still be in place exactly as it existed before, but the way it works internally now has begun to change. It begins to refocus and reshape around, as I like to say, the right people doing the right things with regard to the right initiatives, and the right people helping make the right decisions about the direction for those initiatives and who should be involved in them. Now you are moving to Fluid Form.

In Fluid Form, you don't need the hierarchy and the extensive oversight and control in order to get things done. When you think about it, a hierarchical approach to an organization is a high energy, high cost solution to the basic problem of "How do we get things done around here?" When control and coordination come from within the team, you save a lot of time and money, which translates into getting processes running more smoothly, and ultimately getting products more quickly into an increasingly competitive marketplace.

Ultimately, in Fluid Form, you've got the right people in the right place at the right time—people with a stake in the outcome of a given process, a broader sense of expertise than they would have had if they had remained isolated in their cubbyholes, and ownership of the endeavor. Because they are becoming decision-makers, they are growing as leaders. They are better equipped to decide for themselves if they're on the right track, if something should be stopped, if energy should be redirected, if a plan should be reformulated, or if a process should be repopulated with individuals possessing a different set of skills.

Fluid Form provides far more opportunity to learn, grow, and be successful.

In a Fluid Form organization, there's more of a chance for employees to find uses for their special talents and expertise.

---

2 Ando Ritsuko, *Reuters*, July 8, 2008.

Because Fluid Form is all about creating structures that allow for the right people to be in the right place at the right time, people constantly get new opportunities to develop, to use new skills and talents, and to learn new things. It is important to emphasize this to employees, to get them on board for change.

With Fluid Form, work, in effect, becomes much like going to school. People take different classes and courses. They are engaged in different activities. There's more peer pressure in a hierarchical organization for individuals to stick to their one function, to become narrow specialists excelling in that area, and not to gain broader experience.

In a Fluid Form organization, success is built around what you do, and not so much your place on the org chart. So you don't have the same kind of pressure to specialize. In Fluid Form, the pressure to be successful only by moving up to a new job doesn't exist. That's actually a form of disability within organizations.

Instead, in Fluid Form, your success is based on the kinds of things that you do, who you are and what your talents are, as opposed to where you are in the hierarchy. This is a much more fulfilling approach to work.

In Fluid Form, success breeds success. As the networks grow more successful and people come to rely on them, they see those networks as better ways of managing initiatives, projects, and processes. As a result, they might say, "Hey! We don't even need this extra level of management! We have a hierarchy of four levels— maybe we can get by with just three or two." This allows companies to get more out of their managers, because one manager can now take on strategic roles in fifteen or twenty areas, instead of having to be a hands-on manager in just two or three. That's because those fifteen or twenty projects and initiatives are more self-managing under Fluid Form.

Fluid Form creates more leaders.

People use the word "empowerment" today as if it were a newly invented concept. I saw it in the jungles of Vietnam forty years ago. I would define empowerment as letting people do what they see as the right thing to do, when they need to do it. But when you talk about being effective in combat, you can't wait for the hierarchy and the chain of command to tell you what to do in the heat of battle. It doesn't work. You've got to find a different way to do things. And if you're going to maximize your effectiveness in business or war, you have to empower people down to the lowest level to make decisions, form teams, and get things done without bureaucracy and red tape. This doesn't mean no one is leading. It means building leader-full teams with more people who have leadership skills and confidence to step up to the challenge.

Fluid Form is better organizational engineering—more efficient and effective. It's about engineering a company the right way so that the work gets done the right way. While this seems counterintuitive, the greater degree of the right kind of structure allows for more flexibility and responsiveness.

In this book, you'll find a checklist of things to do in order to create Fluid Form, the steps necessary for your organization to put this methodology into practice. I'll be very clear about what kind of effort is required and what happens in what order. It is my hope that you will take the ideas I offer, extrapolate from them, and make them work for your organization.

Eight steps to establishing Fluid Form in an organization enterprise.

There are stages to this movement. It doesn't happen in one fell swoop. If Fluid Form is introduced in stages, it looks much less like a threatening change project from a consultant or from management that's going to be shoved down everybody's throats. When Fluid Form is introduced gradually, people see the concept as making things work more effectively. It's about simply saying, "Hey, the right people are involved in this from the start." That way, it's not a big change.

The first step to Fluid Form is examining our "as-is" performance. Are we improving or not improving on the major organization and business variables in which we're trying to do well? Often, organizations have that kind of data. That creates the baseline, which is Step One.

Step Two determines where we stand on cultural support. Have we been more rigid, or are we moving more to a collaborative model? What are we doing to make that happen? How even is support throughout the organization? Are we trending ahead? Are we getting better on cultural support for Fluid Form?

Step Three is about processes and linking them with initiatives. Here we create a list of the kind of major processes and sub-processes and how well they're doing, how well they're linked, what the functions are, and what the status is in terms of where we should go and how we can become more process-oriented. It's about determining where we are and where we need to head, and whether we have fallen back relative to that center of gravity, which is to be process- and project-oriented versus functional.

Step Four is removing boundaries. If we're getting more project-oriented, where are the existing boundaries? Can other boundaries be reduced or eliminated? Can we eliminate departments or functions? Can we build stronger relationships across different functions? How do we continue to remove boundaries?

Step Five is the creation of what I call the "virtual home room" that provides all of your people the problem-solving tools they need and the information systems that give them relevant data, so they can see where the project is, what's happening, what needs to be done, and how they need to help. I'll show you how to construct a home room that will become the foundation for supporting your cross-functional teams.

Step Six is weaving networks and flattening the organization. Networks exist to coordinate and manage the various projects' processes. Where are they effective, or not effective? Are they stable, or do they need to be built more robustly? Where do we need new ones? And where are we successful in a way that we might be able to reduce further levels of hierarchy or specific functional management roles?

Step Seven involves reward systems. Are we really rewarding people for doing multiple roles in Fluid Form, or are we not? And what do we need to change to make it work, to make the system more robust?

Step Eight goes to the change of process itself, configuring the Fluid Form Dashboard—which is the refresh button on the web cycle. Here's where we are, here's the new data ... so let's press the refresh button. Where is the energy? Where is the leadership? What do we need to do to keep this moving forward? And how are we approaching the change in the organization? How is it working, and how could it work better? Change is represented by the Fluid Form Dashboard, because the organization is always in movement. A photograph is a snapshot in time of the organization, because the organization itself is not seen as static. Change becomes part of the culture. It's constantly ratcheting up the organization to make it work more effectively.

How does Fluid Form help both internal and external organization consultants?

Whether your job title says "Consultant" or not, if you have sway over the manner in which your organization is run and work is divided, you are indeed an organization consultant. Companies that have developed strong internal consulting groups are knowledgeable and extremely capable of providing the leadership training and facilitation skills that are required for successful change. Because excellent resources already exist for understanding and learning these essentials, this book does not review them. But if you're like many of the consultants I've worked with—both those who are independent operators bearing that title and individuals within organizations whose job it is to create change—you're probably waiting for the next, new thing.

My decades of experience as a consultant make it clear to me that the need for a new approach to reorganization is enormous, and it has literally been decades since a brand-new approach has become available. So if you are a consultant by trade or a "consultant" within your organization, this book is for you.

I am also writing to individuals who must manage units or divisions wherever multi-functional operations take place. This might be a plant manager in a manufacturing facility, or an individual with marketing responsibilities in an organization, or a vice president in charge of R&D. Even though what you do is a function in one sense, you still have many departments and subsets within your overall tasks and you need to integrate your efforts with other functions. If you have anywhere from 500 to 5,000 or more people working for you, then you have all the problems of bureaucracy in trying to make things work better. You're facing all kinds of pressure to reduce costs, to get more output. If anything, in a world of global competition and outsourcing, it's more essential than ever to create organizations that maximize effectiveness. So this book is for you.

The book also is intended for project/process managers, because of all the material you'll find about how to build robust teams. If you've got a project to run involving multiple dimensions or disciplines, and especially if you have complex projects involving different fields in many different areas within your organization, this book is for you. This is especially true if fiefdoms have emerged, and you need a way to tear down the walls that keep your organization from getting things done.

In other words, you don't have to be a CEO or a CFO to benefit from this book and from the Fluid Form concept. You might be an HR director. You might be a director of strategic change, or a senior vice president of strategy. You might be a refinery manager for an oil company. Whatever your organization, whatever problems you face, Fluid Form might just be the answer. So join me, and let's find out whether Fluid Form can help you—and how to make that happen.

Step 1: Where Are You Now?

Assess Your "As-Is": Performance Gaps

The Comanche preferred to march in daylight, but to avoid discovery they would move by the light of the moon ... No European army marched, or could march, with such wilderness skills, such personal discipline, or for that matter, such implicit deadliness.[3]

The Comanche made the finest horsemen of them all ... Other Europeans said that while other Indians rode, Comanches—man, woman and child—had learned to live on horseback. The United Sates soldiers called them the finest light cavalry in the world.[4]

Comanches made use of a loop or thong slipped around the horse's neck from which a rider could hang over the horse's side, shielding himself from hostile bullets or arrows. Only the most skilled horsemen could use this trick, the Comanches quickly became some of the most superb riders who ever lived.[5]

Maybe you're considering Fluid Form Organization because you believe there's an improved "there" out there. Perhaps your organization experienced a recent wake-up call that cost you money or market share. Either way, you may find it valuable to take a step back and assess where you think you are in terms of performance. Where do you currently stand on your most important measures of success?

---

3 Fehrenbach, *Comanches*, 74.
4 Ibid., 94-5
5 Ibid., 96.

Consider how you stack up in areas like these:

- Responding to customers/stakeholders
- Meeting objectives
- Developing focused, measurable initiatives
- Managing key business processes across functions
- Balancing people/skill requirements within budget limitations
- Aligning performance assessment with company goals
- Developing a collaborative culture aimed at improvement

High-level "as-is" scorecarding can itself be a trap. It's easy to fall into "analysis paralysis" as you dig into issues you notice or those dropped on your doorstep. Keep in mind that you are designing a response to the *way* work is done, which is a broader, more comprehensive response than fire-drill types of problem-solving. However, it is pointless to begin a large-scale change effort if the organization goals are not focused, clear, and measurable. Why change anything unless it will make a meaningful contribution?

Otherwise it is simply change for change's sake— and those who say "don't fix it if it ain't broke" have a strong hand to play in this situation. Therefore, it's important to get some ballpark estimate that shows how moving to Fluid Form will make enough difference to justify the time and effort required.

While it may seem challenging to make such an estimate at the outset, the gap defines the rationale for undergoing the painstaking and often stressful process of organization change. For those organizations that really understand the potential of truly effective process and project teams supported by a lean, flexible and flat organization, the size of the gap between current and potential achievement will be larger, and the expectation for performance success as an outcome of the change will be so much the greater.

Where is your organization operating below standard? What areas need to be "ratcheted up"? Whether it's customer support, new product development that crosses functions, reducing the cycle time of products, or leaning out order administration—where are you at in terms of developing your key processes?

What you're really asking is this: in your company, are the right people doing the right things at the right time, or are some people sitting on their duffs? Are you getting the most out of the people you have? In today's world, we are constantly trying to reduce costs and get more out of what we have. We can seek to increase productivity with the people we have now or we can go back to playing one person against the other simply to get ahead. Every company is concerned about that.

If you are developing a collaborative culture aimed at improvement—and most organizations today are trying to be collaborative—then getting the job done and meeting your goals is the most important thing.

Let me share with you an example of superior performance, where an organization came up with really good ideas in regards to changing the effectiveness and fluidity of their manufacturing operations very early on. This is a foundational example of the importance of managing key business processes, building robust teams, and developing cross-functional decision making while flattening the organization.

The organization in question is Procter & Gamble, one of the most admired companies in the world. The story I'm about to share with you will introduce many of the concepts behind Fluid Form—because that's where I learned them.

Inside Procter & Gamble

Fresh out of grad school in the Fall of 1973, I was to be the internal consultant assigned to help Procter & Gamble (P&G)—a very successful (but exceptionally traditional) manufacturing plant—change form to be more like the new, innovative systems that were being built at the time. A sweet, mint-like smell filled the car as I entered the P&G plant in Iowa City. Describing the floors as clean would have been the understatement of the decade. Let's just say, I've eaten off surfaces far less clean! Long rows of machinery provided workspaces for people bottling and packaging familiar consumer products: Scope mouthwash, and Crest and Gleam toothpastes. Not unlike a Navy ship that had readied itself for the Inspector General, I could sense a certain "snap to" attitude everywhere I strolled. People smiled. They were friendly and seemed content as they worked. Conversation was easy, with the common knowledge that Iowa City was one of the most effective plants in the company. Pride dripped off of this community of several hundred, where it was almost a certainty that every employee would someday retire, gold watch in hand.

Though the Iowa City plant was successful as a traditional system within the corporation, P&G was building new pilot plants using non-traditional organization design. Termed "Technician Systems," they were literally built in the green fields of rural areas, far from cities and P&G offices. The rationale? It is far easier to try something new when the old culture, along with its expectations, is far away. Part of the strategy also included creating new plants without union interference and the associated "us vs. them" antagonisms that would discourage the creation of a different way of organizing and building relationships between management and workers.

Iowa City was somewhat under the microscope—it was the first time an attempt was made to transform an existing plant. Teamsters and Steelworkers were a notable presence within Procter & Gamble, and in spite of tremendous efforts to manage conflict and maintain harmony, not all these union/management relationships were the friendliest. Iowa City did have a union, but it was local, not affiliated with any of the big-name nationals. More importantly, the union relationship with management was excellent. Not a single grievance had been filed, a testament to a long history of talking things out. Of course, when you've got a good thing going, that's also a reason not to mess with it.

The new concept, the one being built into the Greenfield Sites, was a novel-at-the-time team-oriented approach at the operator level. This organization could get the job done with fewer people, and those few didn't have "jobs" in the same sense that Iowa City plant employees had jobs. Operators could flow freely, performing the duties of what were previously several jobs—including some duties previously reserved for supervisors. In fact, many of the Technician System plants went beyond job "change," plunging headfirst into eliminating the first level of supervision altogether.

To the many executives and managers (the "P&G for life"-ers), this new system created one hell of a dilemma. The "soft," hands-off look didn't sit right inside a venerable corporation with tried-and-true command-and-control methods. Thankfully, another factor trumped misgivings about the unsettling, upstart system: it was undeniably more productive. In head-to-head comparisons with traditional systems, this seemingly "New Age" approach produced and shipped product for significantly lower costs. In the cutthroat consumer products arena, even the most traditional managers had to kneel at the altar of the bottom line. P&G was sitting on a competitive weapon, so much so that we were told not to discuss their new management approach at conferences outside the company.

The organizing concept was borrowed from British coal-mining experiments in the fifties. Called "socio-technical system design," the general idea was to optimize the way the work technology and humans interacted for best effect. For example, suppose there are three separate jobs on a work team. Traditionally, one individual is responsible for and fulfills only one of those three. On a multi-skill team, all three individuals are capable of fulfilling the work of all three jobs. Even if all three work the same task at a single point to eliminate a critical path bottleneck, they are free to work individually or collectively on any of the tasks in each (or all) of these jobs, *all for the sake of completing the overall work most efficiently.*

The concept, simple. The advantages, obvious. The challenges in making it happen, enormous. The benefits, to quote the MasterCard commercial—priceless.

The role flexibility allows the requirements for getting work done to be more easily met. Individuals have more discretion to respond to conditions within their workplace, because they are able to broaden their contribution with a broader set of tasks. This breeds a greater appreciation for the challenges of the work that others do, a greater understanding of how various tasks must fit together, and ultimately, a greater sense of cooperation—because the work is shared, not owned by one individual. It's not just getting "your" job done ("no flies on me!"). It's about getting our set of tasks done in the most productive way. As a byproduct, researchers found that there was less stress and lower absenteeism among people working under this system.

That's great for the coal miners, but in Iowa City, they did it the old-fashioned way. Everyone had a job with specific duties that only they owned and accomplished, regardless of whether they were overloaded or had spare time. Head operators on each of the product lines were overseers, not necessarily helpers. When there was a mechanical problem, no one could even tighten a bolt: it was time to call for a specialist mechanic (because that was "his job") and take a break. So, while the line was down waiting for the mechanic's arrival, the most knowledgeable head operator could only tap his foot and wait—even if he quickly could have made the small adjustment to get things moving again. This was the way they did it. This was the way it had always worked. No one was uncomfortable with the rules of job ownership, even if, to an outsider, they might appear irrational.

The plant manager, who was comfortable with the same old way, was experienced and, perhaps, intuitive enough to know that there would be pressure down the road to becoming more productive. It was no secret that plans were in the works to build a third sister plant, another of those Greenfield sites, which would almost certainly beat the socks off of Iowa City. Most of the management team sensed the inevitability of change, but I could sense their reluctance. The "shoulds" rang loudly enough for this whole planning endeavor to be chartered and launched, although, of the fifty or so managers and supervisors, only a few were open and upbeat about the possibilities. Most contributed to the effort as they would on any assigned project. After all, they were P&G, and the best of the best. On the side, though, they complained about wasted time that could be spent doing their "real" job.

Even with bottom-line results, the habits and cultural constraints handcuffed the process of planning to make this monumental leap in organizational evolution. We suffered through endless meetings with twenty or more people hashing through a spectrum of big-picture items and, later, levels of detail that seemed minutely unimportant. The marathon mission statement wordsmithing sessions created consensus nightmares among groups with functional overlaps. Guided by a more experienced P&G consultant, I was learning, too—but I was unable to hide my obvious boredom with what seemed to be overly participative and redundant planning.

Early stages of the process were mired in broad abstractions— open systems, equifinality, individual and group core processes—that seemed, at best, only distantly related to the operational tasks. I understood the organizational vernacular from graduate school. Yet I had to agree with the managers that all this seemed more like impractical hogwash invented by the New Age gurus. No wonder, then, that those who had not lived in one of these unconventional beasts complained to each other about these "airy, fuzzy, flaky" endeavors, saying they could be applying all this endless meeting time to real productive work. It was barely possible to not feel badly for the managers, who grudgingly participated at each laborious step, especially when they knew money was being left on the table.

Month after tedious month, we continued to drill down to an agonizing level of detail demanded for the analysis of scores of work processes. Every human task in the bottling, packing, warehousing, and distribution to peripheral elements (such as responding to local agencies) was catalogued by description, skill level, and time to accomplish. Paper piles littered tabletops at these multi-day meetings. And in the meantime, the plant needed running, too.

We had started the planning based on the main mission of the plant and worked our way into the task detail. Yet it soon became evident that once we hit bottom—down as far as we would go in analyzing tasks and work processes—we would be redesigning the work from the "bottom up."

Fast-forward nearly two years. The new organization was finally designed—but still not implemented in the plant! What we had to show for our Herculean effort was the architecture of the organization—*on paper*. With the challenges of garnering enough real support throughout the plant to actually make the change, to steward the abandonment of the sweet base camp of comfort and sell the idea of "new" jobs, we were caging a paper tiger (and a hungry one at that!).

The most formidable objections came from the first line supervisors, many of whom had been promoted up from the operator ranks. Most felt gun-shy at the onset; their position had actually been eliminated in some of the Greenfield sites, somehow divvied up among the newfangled multi-skilled team members. Sure, they were going to retain this first level at Iowa City, but the job—if you could call it a job—was going through a metamorphosis they could not quite grasp, much less become enthusiastic about.

What the supervisors knew of as their job—a job that maybe a parent or relative had held for years, too—was largely going to go away. The traditional oversight and coordination of tasks, including checking the effort and quality of the operators' work, was all going to be embedded in the team. Yes, they still would be involved in assessing performance, but only "involved," not "in charge." They were now supposed to be more "consultative," more of a trainer, responsible for esoteric tasks like boundary management which translated into coordinating with groups outside their team.

The supervisors found themselves in the middle of a career identity crisis. It was pretty clear they were no longer supervising, at least not in the way they knew it nor in the way they had been trained. It sure didn't sound to them like this was a thing of substance—and if it was, it sounded awfully soft and fuzzy, not like a job where you did real work. Comments about a "girl's job" swirled throughout the plant.

I could empathize. They were still supposed to be the "guys in charge" (yes, they were all guys back then). How could they explain who they were to their buddies now?

The plant manager, along with his senior team, listened to the objections and weighed options. Although the new plant was still on the drawing board, they were pummeling their sister plant in Cincinnati. The air of reluctance blended with the perfume-sweet fragrance in the plant, and eventually it brought comfort to their decision not to change, but to stay the course, at least for the present. More than just the discomfort of change itself, supervisors grappled with the story that this was the halfway house: the "superfluous job" between a real job and no job.

The supervisors were right in one respect. They sensed fundamental change, change from the bottom up that broke down the operator hierarchy and a management system that remained unchanged in its hierarchal, "one person to one job" model, to build multi-skill teams.

The socio-technical system was a monumental shift in organizing, but only monumental in the non-management realm. The bottom became flatter, more fluid, more responsive and more capable. There was still a protective pyramid sitting on top that saw no reason to extend the logic to their realm. Work systems that more creatively integrated human abilities around the flow of work competed with the "one person in one job" model and consistently produced superior results.

Meanwhile, on the teams, operators began a progression of learning new skills that allowed them to take on more and more of the total set of tasks for which their team was responsible. The more they learned, the more valuable they were to the team because of their increased flexibility. They were able to take on many of the mechanical adjustment tasks that had been the sole realm of specialists, as well as coordinating tasks formerly owned by the supervisors. More satisfaction, more variety, more challenge and more discretion in a more cooperative environment translated to bigger paychecks and higher productivity. Those coal miners in the fifties had been onto something!

After five or so years, most of the operators had reached the edge of what they could learn. Essentially, they had "consumed" what was the traditional supervisor's job. All the while, the management pyramid remained atop of their innovative system, more observer than full participant. The table was set, but whether management chose to dine was up for grabs. Fresh in their memory was the long, difficult implementation of Phase One with its conflict and ruffled feathers. They also sensed that this might risk their productivity, regardless of the advertised track record of the Greenfield plants.

This competitive organization weapon was only one way to get the job done, they felt, and it was a long, hard road to traverse from traditional roots. Experience suggested it was a lot easier to build one fresh in the Greenfield than take on an arduous renovation. Such a change is tough. It shakes up the box. It goes against the grain.

Five years after Iowa City decided not to make the switch to a socio-technical system, they changed their minds. A new Greenfield site was being built to compete with them directly. The possibility of no longer being the best was enough to force then into the discomfort of making the change after all. The lessons—and the benefits—of Fluid Form were too obvious to ignore.

*

Not every organization goes through such a wrenching change kicking and screaming. In today's world, employees are clamoring for more opportunities to learn and to grow, to burnish their own skills while delivering value for their employers. In today's economy, it's not just businesses that realize they must "grow or go." Employees grasp that same reality in their own careers. So the transition in your organization to Fluid Form will likely be more … well, *fluid* than in the story I just shared with you.

What can be learned from the Procter & Gamble experience? A great deal. Specifically, the organization sought an increase in effectiveness—it analyzed where it was and where it wanted to go. That's Step 1 of Fluid Form. So it built a collaborative culture, which is our Step 2. It then built plants around key business processes— our Step 3. It still maintained the functional organization, but now it built in terms of teams and processes. It reduced boundaries between different groups, for example, combining maintenance, production, and even packaging into one agglomeration. Discrete groups joined together, and the silos were broken down. That's Step 4.

Next, it built multifunction teams within the silos—and trained people for many roles horizontally. The company built those teams very robustly, with the flexibility to match resources to needs. The company taught its people leadership skills. That's Step 5. As a result, it was able flatten the organization and take out one, or even two, layers of management. Decision-making became flatter. That's Step 6.

They changed the reward system and now rewarded people for doing what they were doing as part of teams—not just based on their own positions in the org chart. That's Step 7. And finally, they never settled for where they were, but kept growing. They ratcheted things up and then ratcheted them up some more. That's Step 8. As a result, Procter & Gamble enjoyed productivity gains of *35 to 40 percent.*

That's Fluid Form in action. Now that you've got a baseline for your company or division, and a sense of where you can go, let's move to Step 2, building a collaborative culture. The remarkable thing is that this is what your employees have probably wanted all along.

Step 2: Assess Your Cultural Support for Membership Fluidity

On the surface, hunting band society was a pure democracy of adult males, who made all the great decisions—peace, war, alliance, migration— around the council fire ... Their procedure was ruled far more rigidly by centuries of custom than any modern parliament is governed by rules of order.[6]

The Comanche law was not a complex, rationalized thing, which could be changed by the decision of emperors, judges or parliaments at will, and which at times could be understood fully only by trained elites. The People's law consisted of their conventional wisdom, accreted by painful experience. No individual or council could set such custom-law aside: every chief or council made decisions that all the People immediately understood.[7]

Most companies have learned to build process and project team infrastructure sufficient to provide focus, direction and support from one or more managers outside of the team and further up the hierarchy. In moving to Fluid Form, it's important to be clear about the approach to leadership, decision-making, how people will work together, and what's expected of individuals and teams. Where is your organization currently in terms of cultural support for fluidity?

Your assessments in the following categories will represent a thumbnail of how work is done in your organization and ultimately shape the extent to which Fluid Form can be concretely practiced and cultivated. Commitment to building a strong, process-based

---

6 Fehrenbach, *Comanches*, 44.
7 Ibid., 46.

organization with significant employee involvement and flexibility in defining and redefining jobs goes hand-in-hand with building Fluid Form capability. So let's begin.

- Employee Knowledge: What level of knowledge are employees expected to have about the organization's objectives in relationship to their job?

- On-the-Job Learning: To what degree are employees expected to learn on the job, or to expand their skills to other job areas?

- Collaboration: What is the expected balance between independent work and collaborative work within or across teams?

- Process Orientation: To what extent is the organization focused on work processes and their improvement, rather than compartmentalized by job, department, and/or function?

- Job Flexibility: How will the organization allow for the design or redesign of jobs versus strictly adhering to strict job descriptions? How easily can employees work outside of the confines of their job descriptions?

- Individual Input: How much are people involved in providing input to their operational area? Do they have the freedom to make independent decisions for the benefit of the business?

- Voice in Change: How much say do people have in designing the change(s) and in being a part of the transition to an improved organization?

You also want to ask yourself the following key questions: How could this type of cultural change move forward? How big a cultural shift will you need to make? Which aspects of it will you need to work on? Where do anticipate resistance, and what is your plan to overcome it?

Employee Knowledge

Over the years, it has become more common to expect that employees know what the business goals are and how the work and the efforts of their team fit in terms of achieving those goals. Some organizations don't teach their employees how their jobs tie into the ultimate business goals. Many times, the attitude in management is:"Here's your job, just do it." Companies that train and educate all members about the relationship of their operation to business goals are in place to operate at a higher level of performance. They are a culture that is more ready for Fluid Form.

On-the-Job Learning

In Fluid Form, employees are responsible for learning new skills and volunteering for assignments and education that bring growth. In other words, there is a cultural expectation that people will want to take on more. Those who take on more and learn more also can contribute more when the situation calls for those skills. Operations that have greater flexibility and can shift resources to meet changing demands fit better into the Fluid Form approach.

Collaboration

Are employees expected to remain in their office and do work on their own, or is it acceptable and expected to collaborate and team up as needed to be more innovative and efficient? Are your employees comfortable working together, especially outside of their department or function? It's critical for the culture to encourage, even demand, that individuals or teams get out of their silos and communicate with other units when coordination is necessary. This is a cornerstone, the most important and essential of these dimensions for cultural support of Fluid Form.

Process Orientation

Are you compartmentalized? Does each person have one job with one set of tasks? Or are they expected to work outside of their job description, outside of their function on project and process teams? Is the majority of work completed within departments or functions? Are key business processes identified and are people with the right skills and information staffing them? Are they being fully utilized and making a difference in the success of the business?

Job Flexibility

How easy is it to work outside of the confines of a specific and narrow job description? Can the job change over time? Is it okay to take on different assignments, and to work on a number of project or process teams? Are members open to flexible sets of tasks across a spectrum of roles that would shift based on the needs of the business?

Individual Input

How much are people involved in providing input to their operational area? Again, are you welcoming new ideas and encouraging innovative thinking? Is there an expectation in your culture for members of the organization to come up with new ideas and better ways of functioning? How much freedom do they have to make independent decisions for the benefit of the business? Do they always have to go up the hierarchy in order to get approval on action items? Are they trusted, within the work that they are doing or the process they are involved in, to contribute and make decisions that are good decisions? If someone makes a wrong decision, are they reprimanded, or do you say, "Hey, you should have done it differently, but it's great that you went ahead and took an action— because taking action is important as long as it's based on your best understanding of the situation at the time." Do employees take the initiative to provide input?

Voice In Change

How often do you hear people voice opinions on how things could be run differently or more effectively? Does your organization welcome those opinions? Are your employees comfortable and confident in voicing their ideas? And when there is change in process, how involved are all members of your organization in making that change happen successfully? If your company welcomes change and works together to support, incorporate and make transitions easily and painlessly, then you are well on your way to a Fluid Form operation. If you work in a culture that's still fairly fifties oriented— a narrow-minded and bureaucratic model in which you sit at your desk, do what you're told, and don't ask any questions—the distance to Fluid Form will be greater.

Successful organizations encourage a process-based emphasis with significant employee involvement and flexibility. You need the culture to build these teams and you also need the right people on the teams, fully engaged. In order for your teams to be fluid and flexible, you will want the capability to move people in or out of different teams and to be able to alter what they are working on.

Is your culture perpetuating a flexible attitude among members? This is a major component to Fluid Form organizations. Putting processes in place is one part, but you need members—actual people—to carry the processes out effectively. Envision cultural support of membership fluidity as a checklist of what needs to happen in order to develop Fluid Form.

Inside General Electric

In the previous chapter, we examined how Procter & Gamble had adopted a well-thought out systems approach to building innovative organization, which most noticeably changed operations at the bottom. Let's now see how another of America's most respected enterprises, General Electric, created a more dramatic, fast, and intentionally not-heavily-engineered initiative. They made the transition more than a decade later than P&G, in the late eighties. This account will illustrate the concept of changing the culture to become more fluid.

General Electric's CEO, Jack Welch, had already made a name for himself by selling off any GE business unable to be either 1st or 2nd in its market. Having made it clear that being at the top was the only acceptable score, GE then launched their own home-grown program to upgrade the performance of all their businesses.

Welch's idea of making businesses more competitive by improving organization performance was more of a "microwave" version of P&G's. He started at the top, without the detail, complexity or extensive time commitment of socio-technical system design. Jack's goal of preventing managers from micro-managing—not giving their subordinates the space to do their work—started with eliminating a level of management. For this initiative, a business manager comfortable with the buffer of five or six direct reports would have to take on all their reports directly, which often totaled more like eighteen! Without the time to hover over each, the more relevant business issues, which were generally cross-functional in nature, would rise to the top of the to-do list.

This "forced flattening" also encouraged managing more broadly across the organization instead of only hammering down on subordinates. The policies and procedures that sometimes led to eighteen levels of approval before a decision could be made joined the list of unnecessary work that needed to be eliminated. The goal: emphasize working across the boundaries of function and geography to solve the problems that would help the business become successful, and de-emphasize (read: eliminate) the preoccupation with managing the mundane tasks assigned to subordinates within a given function.

This was not the only hammer to fall. The most important product of this strategy of decisiveness and action was forcing managers to actively engage with the workforce to solve problems together. It was called "Work-Out" and it was a monumental cultural shift. Welch had a well-earned a reputation for downsizing operations, but his mangers complained that, while he was effective in getting people out, he hadn't reduced the workload they left behind. The fewer remaining folks still had the same-sized elephant to eat. In response to this legitimate concern, Work-Out focused upon eliminating useless, time-consuming tasks.

I joined the team of consultants hired to lead the change effort at GE. We were a network of Organization Development practitioners, linked together by past work projects and a similar, participative but task-oriented approach to change. My first Work-Out in the GE Plastics Division felt like a trip in a time machine—unfortunately, a trip back to the fifties! Managers rarely spoke to their employees, much less asked their opinion about anything. They avoided each other with a level of hostility that surprised me for a company so long established and so well regarded. GE was light-years behind Procter & Gamble in terms of developing participation and harvesting the gains from that kind of relationship. Ironically, there seemed to be a level of comfort with the anger managers and workers held for each other, a standoff that made anything that didn't work well someone else's fault.

Work-Out meant that management and the workforce would engage in small teams to take on meaningful but quickly solvable problems (termed "low-hanging fruit") and, yes, work on them together to solve them. The result was to get rid of work that wasted time and energy and to find ways to do the right work more efficiently. Far from being a complex reengineering program, Work-Out was directly aimed at building positive participation across the management/worker boundary in the quest for a more productive operation. The problems were selected, for the most part, as cross-functional, to promote working across functional barriers to get the important stuff done.

The hammer to join in was here, too. While volunteerism was encouraged, the level of distrust made conscription the option *du jour* for managers who valued their career. Jack's train was on a roll, which meant it was better to be on it than to be waiting at the station. Even with anticipation and somewhat passive resistance, the desired result could be a culture more eager to work across the functional boundaries by building ad hoc teams when necessary to solve problems. Clearly, the blame gaming and finger-pointing between groups wasn't working. This was about building energy to get things done. And it required the trust that, on the other side of the functional fence, there would be similar enthusiasm.

Instead of trying to solve all the product returns problems, the team would pick five or six, out of scores of issues—five or six that, if solved, would make some impact on the problem. The whole point was to get something done that made a visible difference. If they had tried to work the entire array of associated issues, lack of progress and lack of any success would have the reverse effect of de-energizing and souring team members on "just another" management charade.

Sure, the standard set of problem areas appeared on the list, from quality, cost reduction, material supply and cycle time—but the overarching principle was to "slice and dice," to find within each of those spots where wasted time and effort could be identified and pulled out. The time boundary was to only pick those areas that could be solved and implemented in less than ninety days, which meant there would be a visible end to the project, a reassurance that this would not be an endless, and perhaps useless, effort.

Early topics were focused and simple, such as "How can we reduce the cost on the XX spring mount by 10 percent?" or "How can we improve the uptime on the YY mixer within 90 days?"

It was no surprise that my team contributed more than their fair share of yelling and screaming. "This was just another management ploy to eliminate jobs," "You're the hired gun for management," and "We've been down this path and management's done nothing!" became common battle cries. The few managers on the team would counter with examples of worker resistance to change past practices. It was a refrain that kept recurring as we pushed ahead to slice and dice, trying to pick a few areas where there was a sense of wasted effort and come up with ideas to make it work better.

Unlike most of my prior consulting, I felt tremendous pressure to make my team successful. They would be presenting their results in front of all the other teams (sometimes as many as fifteen) to the higher level Decision-Making Group. I had only two days to work with them. Encouraging participation and simultaneously driving through the basic problem-solving steps to action plans was no small challenge. Was I a consultant or a typical manager on a deadline, worried about how I would look when the time came for my team to show their stuff? It was stressful. I became driven. I pushed, begged, cajoled and worried all the way through.

The ideas were generally not revolutionary. Things like "move a work table to the other side of the room to save a step or two" were representative of the types of suggestions. Still, they were more than idle suggestions. They were do-able, low-hanging fruit ideas, and each made a difference in the overall scheme of things. At the end of two days, we had boiled things down to about twenty-five action plans for members of the team to accomplish within the ninety-day window.

A key element in all this was the team members making it happen, rather than throwing it over the transom for some other group to do. Others outside the group might be asked to help, but someone on the inside had to drive it. Ownership was a key component.

In the next phase, each of the many teams reported out to a Management Decision-Making Team that would give the thumbs-up or thumbs-down for each of the action plans. What cemented the process were the monthly follow-up sessions, when congratulations were delivered. It is from this point on until completion that most participative systems fail to deliver.

What was different about this decision-making process, compared to past practices, was the cross-functional composition of this team. It included stakeholder representation from all the functions affected by any action taken within the teams. This established a decision-making alternative to traditional "send it up the hierarchy" without full representation. Validating that a team's plan was in the right direction and important to the business, along with sufficiently broad management commitment to effectively support the follow-through, meant that the work was completed and the results were achieved.

Jack Welch appeared at my first report to bless the process and impress everyone with its importance to the business. To his credit, he asked tough questions of the teams, challenging some to come up with better solutions. More memorable was how he challenged managers on the decision-making team, who had endless, logical reasons not to support an action plan, especially when the central rationale was that we had "always done it that way." His charisma and high energy was transformational. Work-Out was changing the culture. These cross-functional teams were doing what they were supposed to do—getting things done. Best of all, management was supporting them. Beyond the circus-like atmosphere of these giant report-out meetings, smaller groups were forming on their own to solve problems without waiting for the big event. This was working.

To reinforce the practical application of Work-Out, Jack altered the definition of success for managers. Historically, the company rewarded only results, regardless of the organizational turmoil created along the way. Results remained the dominant focus, but they now had to be achieved with the right management process of involvement. Getting results while traumatizing the workforce was now considered the same failure as not getting results used to be. You had to have it both ways to be a Star. While it seemed at first that the hammer was coming from above, the focus was to engage across the functional stovepipes.

Cross-functional management leadership was critical to creating and maintaining this new action-oriented culture. But the management pressure was also to flatten the top of the organization and force cross-boundary collaboration to solve the problems that blocked performance. Overall participation and dialog between management and employees increased. The top pulled the bottom into the game, and the employees learned that bringing up problems and being part of solving them could actually be fun. Even as a consultant, I had fun seeing action taken and results achieved so quickly.

While GE flattened from above and pressed for cross-functional problem solving and decision-making—the beginnings of network management—P&G had crafted highly tuned, multi-function teams that brought isolated job functions together, which is the genesis of robust teams. Both were focused on getting work done more efficiently by more fully utilizing the talents and energy of their human resources. The different approaches are two important puzzle pieces, benchmarks along the path to a new concept of organizing that builds on their innovative success.

Welch's approach: first flatten the organization, and then try to create fluidity. My experience teaches me that things work better the other way around: first create process stability and effective networks, and then flatten the organization. In Step 3 in the next chapter, I'll show you how to get that started.

Step 3: Assess Your "As-Is":

Project/Processes & Functional Initiatives

Since the war society of the Comanche was fluid, and there was no permanent military rank or privilege of leading men at war, any proven warrior might lead a war party if he presented the proper medicine. A warrior became trail chief by convincing his potential followers, through his explanations of his visions, that he had made powerful medicine.[8]

Convinced of strong medicine, the Comanche war band took the trail at the crest of a manic wave, fearsome as ravening wolves. (p.72-73) Hunter warriors cooperated like a pack of wolves, running behind a crafty leader.[9]

Our conditioned conception of organization is the pyramid chart with ever increasing boxes as you move downward until "my job" appears in one of the boxes. Work is then seen as a set of activities that belong to an individual or to a unit/department.

Perhaps there is another way to conceive of work. Suppose you started a new business. Instead of hiring humans as employees or contractors, your organization would be populated by Droids. Think of Droids as employees that perform only the work required when it is needed. What sort of organizational structure would be required to support this? Would a traditional hierarchal system make sense? Let's use this analogy to explore the tension between mechanistic effectiveness and the human need for success, which are often channeled into "moving up the hierarchy."

---

8 Fehrenbach, *Comanches*, 70.
9 Ibid., 44.

Imagine a Droid warehouse with a sufficient quantity of skilled Droids as the sole source for the "folks" doing what heretofore would have been the province of human activity. Humans require a certain level of income to live and a host of human needs for interaction, accomplishment, performance feedback and career fulfillment, but these Droids require none of that. Score one for the Droids. In fact, the Droids would only be called out of the warehouse to do the actual work needed, at just the time it is needed, whether it be individual work, group tasks or Droid-to-Droid engagement to determine the best time and place for coordinated activity. Once their specific tasks are completed, they return to the warehouse and go "offline." In fact real life Droids are more than fictional today. Honda has upgraded its "humanoid" robot to allow it to interact with other robots and to work together. Information about the current status of each robot is shared with other networked units, which enable the robots to complete tasks more efficiently.

Hey, this Droid thing is sounding pretty good! "Let's hurry up and go build some widgets or something," you may be saying. Imagine the efficiency! Imagine the results! Imagine not feeling pressured to buy school raffle tickets or Girl Scout cookies! (Well, okay, let's keep the cookies.) Simply stated, the activity is focused only on the work required. Apart from the Droids doing the work, various Droids might move in and out of the warehouse, from inactive to active to inactive state. Work is completed by individuals Droids or groups, as needed. Depending upon the nature of the business, you might see varying degrees of "movement."

Let's assume the role of Droid Resources (or Organizational Droid-velopment!) and describe this Droid organization. What sort of organization chart (if any) would you draw? Hmmm, the Droid organization is about movement and work, but not about the static dimensionality of hierarchy and function. Think about it. Putting a classical organization chart around the Droid operation quickly becomes an absurd way of characterizing both what it is and how it functions.

Establishing (or at least fantasizing) that this Droid organization would be remarkably efficient, what conclusions might we draw for organizations today? Well, organizations achieve greater efficiency when focusing on key processes to coordinate workflow. Doesn't this sound exactly like what we created in Droidville? Today, we strive to achieve the efficiency of the Droids by creating horizontal work processes, but this is all being done within the hierarchal, functional organization, which divides work into departments and jobs—all managed neatly within the hierarchy.

By its very nature, the work process "sees" horizontally. The modern organization "controls" vertically, but sometimes tries to stretch the horizontal to get better results. Given the inherent tension, there must be something extremely compelling about the walls of hierarchy and function to make this form endure. Droids emote neither happiness nor unhappiness with their work situation. But as humans, we have *our* needs, which are manifested in concert with the environment that surrounds us. The modern organization "creates its own weather" in the sense that its hierarchal nature activates our need to be successful and channels it into "moving up the hierarchy." Thus, while we might find the work itself fulfilling and the people we are working with a wonderful community who meet our social needs, the status ladder in our face is far too compelling to ignore.

How many leaders would it take to run the Droid organization? Perhaps none. If the Droids could think on this dimension, what would they want or require in terms of coordination or leadership to help them do a better job than they are doing today? They might collectively become the coordinating network that choreographs their individual effort. In fact, in the last several decades, we have created many organizational situations in which the leadership functions are carried out in "leaderless" units.

Similar to our Droid analogy, a Fluid Form organization would be characterized by a vast field of Fluid Form teams, projects and networks coordinated and managed without the visible presence and force of significant hierarchy. As you read on, think about whether you—or others accustomed to being leaders—could find success in ways other than moving up the ladder. Reflect back to project teams you have been on in your life. What roles did you play? Were you ever a team leader? Did you experience membership changes as a project progressed? Did your role ever shift over time? What made the difference between having a good or a dreadful experience? Ever wish you were working with Droids instead of people? Tell the truth!

In a Fluid Form organization, the "work" becomes steps in a process of making the product or producing the service, instead of individual jobs and clusters of people doing a certain category or type of work. Instead of thinking about how to classify jobs or organize departments to do the work, let's think about how to combine individual skill sets to do the work most efficiently. We tend to think that we have to develop functions and hierarchy in an organization, but when you are truly process-oriented, you don't think about that first. What you think about first is who can do the work, how can they do it, how do they interact with each other, and what skills do they need collectively to complete the job? Now you are describing the work processes themselves without regard to jobs, people or structure. It's a case of working from the inside-out versus the antiquated, inefficient top-down.

For example, if a packaging factory's main assignment was to package Frisbees, the core work process would be:

1. Forklifts take boxes of Frisbees and display packs from the warehouse to the assembly area;

2. Boxes of both are emptied;

3. Display packs are folded and individual Frisbees put in each display pack;

4. Completed packs are then repacked in boxes of clusters of 20;

5. Boxes are taken back to the warehouse by forklift to await shipment.

In a traditional organization, a department might exist for each of the five steps, with the employees in that department trained only in that one skill, doing only that one task. But one department could be overloaded, desperately needing help, while another stood idle, waiting for work to do. In a multi-skilled, process-centered organization, individuals would have learned two or more of those skills and would be continuously engaged doing the right set of tasks at the right time for maximum productivity.

Going back to the view of an organization of Droids—not people with jobs—the most efficient set of steps or activities to make and package the product is the operational goal. This process can only be implemented and improved by people if they understand the process requirements that they must then organize around. Most organizations today have a mix of functional and process initiatives.

To get an idea of how you're doing at what you do, first ask: what exactly is it that you do? Rethinking your organization through Fluid Form eyes, you will first need to take an inventory and list key Initiatives, Processes, Projects, Activities (Councils, Committees, etc.). Simply stated, what works together and what doesn't?

Here are the questions to ask:

- What do you have in place already in terms of process, projects and activities?

- Which of those are major processes and which of those are working well and already are oriented correctly?

- Which of those have good coordination and have the right depth of experience and people on them?

- And how well are they working with their stakeholders and other important people to get the job done?

Many organizations begin to take inventory, but they fail to see the entire scope of their performance. They tend to focus on functional performance rather than linking related functional and process activities and objectives.

Identify and assess your functional initiatives:

- Are they too specialized?

- Are they too centralized?

- Are some functions undermining processes?

- Is there adequate coordination of activities across functions?

- Are the right people involved? Should people in other functions be involved?

- Are the right stakeholders involved for quick decision-making and support?

- Should your functional initiatives be more process-oriented?

What we're really asking are these crucial questions: How well are your processes and functional initiatives linked? How thick and insular are the functional silos?

Next, with the list, describe the links of any related components to determine:

- Level of interdependence
- Coordination required
- Potential synergy or conflict

You will probably find that many of the functional initiatives need to become more process-oriented. It doesn't mean that they all have to be set up to be cross-functional, but should they be more inclusive? In order to really be effective, you will need to get a handle on all of the work and determine the extent of process development that makes the most sense in achieving your objectives.

Let's look at a story about a company that was suffering from functional fragmentation, and see how identifying and changing their functional initiatives and processes saved the organization.

Inside "StorServ, Inc."

Sometime after Silicon Valley had grown from semiconductors to software—but before the Internet bust—a struggling company we'll call StorServ, Inc. made network storage servers. Network storage servers are basically boxes that contain the hardware and software to store vast amounts of data that can be made available to people on a network when they need it. When this company sent up a flare for assistance, it was with a clear sense of urgency and nervousness.

As a consultant, I must confess that I've always preferred calamitous situations. There's usually a built-in urgency in those situations that makes it easier to get the right people engaged.

In this case, their business situation was brutally clear: another company was about to steal their lunch and eat it in front of them, too. A competitor was coming out with a new server in six months that had performance and features which would surely obsolete StorServ's current product. They had been leapfrogged, and they knew that none of their customers would still be their customers six months down the road unless they had something better or comparable to offer.

Although a new product was in the works, the typical development product rollout history was nine months from concept to product, which would not be fast enough for anything but second place. In this market, that could mean "first loser." In fact, with a little prodding, I found out that the nine-month rollout was really more like thirteen months. To add insult to injury, on this go around, they put a stake in the ground at a five-month development cycle: a big declaration, but a wobbly one, without a clear and notably improved plan. There was a pervasive sense of gloom that the company would surely go under, sending several thousand employees out to hit the bricks.

The company was functionally fragmented into many different departments. Though hardware and software made up the two main engineering groups, many more technical pockets with similarly skilled specialists were scattered throughout the organization. The new product, as an extension of the old, needed new features and a higher level of performance to meet the next competitive bar. The construction of these new features, however, could not easily be accomplished without dialog and tradeoffs among the specialist pockets. Making this happen across the functional boundaries—without major delays—had been a longstanding challenge.

Before I arrived, they had settled on a well-intended, last-ditch approach. They had formed twenty-five cross-functional teams composed of hardware and software engineers, sprinkled with a dash of marketing, operations and finance. This approach is not revolutionary. Indeed, cross-functional teams are a common organizational method for getting the right people together to deal with interrelated issues in the same time and space. It's a practical attempt to provide the critical mass necessary to get something done.

Each team was charged with building one of the features as part of the new product architecture. On paper, it looked as though they were positioned to take a run at the accelerated schedule—except for one small detail. None of the teams had a member with experience leading a team like this. In fact, the executives in charge admitted they were uncertain that more than a couple of individuals across the entire organization possessed the skills necessary to lead a team successfully.

My mission, if I chose to accept it, was to conduct whatever training was required to ensure that each of the teams would do their job in this compressed timeframe for generating a new product. The objectives for these teams were steeped in numbers or percentages associated with features such as speed, availability, resiliency, scalability and connectivity cost. For engineering milestones in one feature team, there might be trade-offs or choices another team would have to adjust to—or perhaps block, in favor of their own objective. This process is typical of what you would expect to contend with across interdependent teams as they weigh choices and negotiate tradeoffs in the interests of building the best overall product.

Pulling my head out of the lion's mouth, I crafted a quick, practical training program with four hours allocated to each team to build project capability. While this seemed hugely unrealistic, given the leadership gap, doing something quickly appealed to the side of me that favors doing and moving forward over debating the finer points while missing the opportunities. Given the time limitations, I concluded that doing and training had to be one in the same; I had four hours to build a fully functioning project team or bust.

The four-hour agenda was 90 percent standard practice plus one unusual idea for dealing with the lack of leadership talent. The standard planning steps included:

- Objectives—the specifics of the feature(s) to be developed
- Boundaries—what was inside and outside of the team's scope
- Technical Hurdles—engineering issues that might be difficult to achieve
- Cross-Team Issues—interdependencies with other teams
- Resources—sufficient technical talent on, or available to, the team
- Action Planning and Timelines
- Project Leadership Allocation

It was this last element of the planning agenda that would make the difference between success and failure. Knowing what to do and having the technical talent is sufficient only if they can work together under time pressure successfully and, just as importantly, coordinate and negotiate tradeoffs with the other teams.

Only two or three of the teams were lucky enough to have seasoned engineers that had run projects before and seemed comfortable with taking on this mantle for their team. The rest of the teams—which did, indeed, have smart young engineers—worked diligently through the first six steps of the build agenda, but they did so with that dazed look that suggested they didn't believe this "leaderless" team would ever pull off their assignment.

In the final step, I provided each team with a ten-point assessment focused on the basic leadership requirements for projects (see figure on page 50). The team members filled it in, and we took a poll on each item. The averages were in the 1 to 2 range. The dazed look turned into one of gloom. It was worse than they'd thought. Everyone hunkered down, hoping not to get picked as the team "leader," the one who would take the blame for failure, the one whose career would receive the black mark. I couldn't blame them. Who volunteers to be Chief Deck Chair Arranger on the *Titanic*?

It was time for a reframe: instead of considering the leadership function as something for which one person must take complete responsibility, we looked at each of the ten items individually and discussed who on the team felt they could successfully manage a single aspect of the team leader responsibility. Doors opened, and gloom turned to possibility. Very quickly, volunteers emerged who felt they had the skills and interest to manage one, two, or even three items.

For most teams, several people combined their abilities to own the list of ten. The leader was not one, but three or four people. More importantly, there was a confidence that the *leader work* could get done sufficiently for the team to accomplish its objectives.

The mood in the teams almost universally transformed from "down and doubt" to "yes, we might just pull this off." Isn't that the point? The outcome was the feeling that this dispersal of project leadership responsibilities might work adequately enough. It would have been impossible to train individual leaders to do it all in the compressed time frame. Ironically, the very *lack* of capable leaders allowed for this unorthodox solution.

Team Assessment

1 No Ability	2 Needs Improvement	3 Adequate	4 Competent	5 Outstanding
How Well Do We				
1. Define Key Issues				1 2 3 4 5
2 Prioritize Key Issues				1 2 3 4 5
3. Develop Solutions				1 2 3 4 5
4. Decide on Critical Actions				1 2 3 4 5
5. Determine Responsibility for Assignments & Action Plans				1 2 3 4 5
6. Accept Accountability for Individual Assignments				1 2 3 4 5
7. Stay on top of all Team project Variables				1 2 3 4 5
8. Maintain Critical Interface Relationships.				1 2 3 4 5
9. Build Confidence				1 2 3 4 5
10. Build Energy & Momentum				1 2 3 4 5
OVERALL RATING:				1 2 3 4 5

Larger questions remain. Is leading and coordinating a job with a defined skill set, or is it an array of skills that can be separated into units and assigned to an individual as simply one of many tasks that defines one's work on a team? We do not normally consider shared leadership as a practical approach. Is that because it is inherently inferior to having individuals who encompass this entire skill and task set, or simply that our hierarchal universe is accustomed to and comfortable with having single leaders? Is the requirement to demonstrate leadership skills in order to move up the ladder also a propelling factor, both for individuals to seek the opportunity and for organizations to provide it, to test for capability?

Although optimistic, this was no time to break our arms patting ourselves on the back. The job was far from done. The newly formed teams at least believed they could coordinate their internal work, but accomplishing the larger objective of shortening the product development timeframe remained a dreamlike fantasy. Once the teams were formed and it became clear that these chosen few would be spending the majority of their time in team mode vs. their comfortable and recognizable functional jobs, this loose network seemed more like a ship leaving port. The new group disconnected from the stable, functional organization that spawned it.

This happened, in part, because only one Director linked the network back to the mother ship, by spending a small portion of his time visiting and monitoring. The lack of encouragement and support was noticeable after the launch—clearly not a best practice—which only served to create a deepening sense of isolation.

Getting the job done inside each team was challenge enough. Negotiating the overlapping issues across teams posed another leadership challenge, at a higher level. After discussing with each team who could help coordinate these ongoing issues, typically two or three individuals would emerge with sufficient skills or interest among them to collectively take on what no single person had the skill or confidence to accomplish alone.

It was surprising to all involved that the teams did meet with each other and were able to work out practical compromises in the interests of the larger objective.

Despite the ability to move forward and handle differences without the delays and hang-ups expected, there remained a pervasive disbelief that the new product could be developed anywhere close to this unrealistic, five-month deadline. Call it "lifeboat syndrome," but just as disbelief lurked on the fringes, a new culture was emerging within this network.

Things were getting done quickly, effectively. Benchmarks and timelines were being met. Engineers talked about how they were solving the technical problems with each other, how they were becoming energized to stay on task and move forward without the usual delays and second-guessing from managers above them. Instead of slogging through the day with an incremental sense of accomplishment, they were moving more effortlessly in and out of the tasks that propelled their team and the larger network toward the objective. They started talking about how much more they liked being in this organization, how much more effective they were, and how positive they felt about their accomplishments.

Time passed quickly, as it often does when things are clicking; three-and-a-half months had passed since these teams were formed. They did it! It was magic. Not only had they beaten their "unrealistic" goal of five months, they also absolutely destroyed the previous best of thirteen. It was a stay of execution for the company, and a fairly joyous one at that. They would beat the competitors to the marketplace, and more importantly, save all those jobs. The icing on the cake was these folks' "trial by fire" had led their way into what could be called an organizational evolution. A high payoff win-win.

Had they traveled for a brief time to an alternate organization universe? Had they done something very unusual by providing "good enough" leadership and project skills in a uniquely shared way, without the talent typically required? Or did they stumble into a collective talent pool that we don't often tap into? Were there synergies added to the project beyond the summation of these skills, energy and enthusiasm, that benefited the project beyond an unorthodox approach to leadership?

It didn't happen just by tossing people together into teams. Detailing and assigning specific project-coordination roles among the members built a structural robustness to meet the unthinkable challenge. And all this was largely accomplished in less than a day, without experienced leaders, without extensive training, and in a climate without much support.

For a time, they lived in a fluid organization where the network was the primary coordinating mechanism and where the skills available were maximized toward an objective. Although many talked about wanting to stay in this mode, it wasn't long before they returned to their functional roles. Maybe they had needed the adversity to give them permission to get "out of the box." Five years later, the company was acquired by a competitor.

Let's take a look at another company that was able to feel the successes of Fluid Form, and how they were doing without it.

Inside Intel

In the early 1990s, Intel was frustrating its customers. It took 65 days from the time an order was placed to let the customer know when they would receive it. Of course, this made their customers' planning a nightmare.

The process to solve this dilemma and reduce the 65-day wait to less than 10 was to develop a more capable end-to-end IT solution. Many existing planning levels needed to be integrated. Long-range planning was looking ahead more than three years. Division marketing was focused one year out. Tactical planning was looking out several months. Fabrication and Assembly planning were far more immediate. All were operating on different systems that did not interact. There was also geographic dispersion. Fabrication was in other states, and Assembly was in the Far East.

A team with mostly IT staff was commissioned to pull the pieces together with a system that could accurately forecast delivery time far more quickly than the existing 65 days. Their own schedule was to complete the process and have the new system functional in six months. Part of the challenge was the developers' difficulty getting data from the various planning groups, because they were busy and operating in different locations and in different time frames. The six months went by. Another six months was added to the schedule. Before another six months could be added, the project was put on hold. Speeding up delivery was an extremely important effort that, like many others, languished because the company could not focus the right people long enough to be successful.

After more than a year of no progress on the Intel IT system, I was summoned to meet with a team made up of representatives from all the planning areas. We came together for three days, which started off with a blame-fest and little hope of compromise, as each functional planner held to their unique way of reporting, based on vastly different time horizons.

When there is enough time to sort through all the parameters and possibilities, enough common ground can be found to get results. They hammered out a raw but consensus-friendly approach, involving a combination of calling and faxing, to be integrated on one spreadsheet. It worked. The 65-day wait to forecast delivery went down to five days, almost immediately.

This group of about fifteen was stunned by their success and equally perturbed that they had not had a workable system for so long, when the solution had been right in front of them. The automated IT system was built on this hand-crafted process and was up and running within a few months.

After getting the job done, it seemed obvious that this practical process had been the best way to solve the problem. Yet, why does this successful approach happen so infrequently? Why is it that creating teams to get important work done so often dissolves into the same ineffective, bureaucratic blur that happened the first time around?

The answer may lie in the presumption that more is better when it comes to information. There's a myth out there that the higher volume of data always lead to faster and better problem-solving and decision-making—and the more complex, the better. The large organizations of today would stymie those from the traditional fifties with what looks like a constant cross fire of information overload, meetings, conflicting demands, and the ongoing stress of finding balance on a playing field where balance is often just a momentary pause before the inevitable engulfment. There are several factors that consistently create this unsavory stew.

We've talked a lot about creating projects, processes and functional initiatives, and we have begun to take a look at which ones are process-oriented. Now it's time to put them all on the table and ask, "Which of these are linked? Which ones should go together? What's the level of interdependence between them? What's the coordination required? Where is there synergy or conflict?"

Why should we do this? Well, organizations often have functional initiatives in place whose purposes do cross. Cross-functional processes, however, are often out of tune with functional initiatives.

Years ago, the university I attended built a number of new structures. Instead of pouring sidewalks when they had finished, they waited until after the next winter, when the paths that students naturally took had been clearly beaten across the lawns. Actual behavioral practice—usually the shortest/smartest distance between two points—became the blueprint for building paths in those footsteps.

So, the main question to answer is: What's the right alignment? Often, the organization is putting too much work into things that aren't really woven together correctly. In order to really be effective, you will need to get a handle on all of the work and determine what processes make the most sense in achieving your objectives, as well as what boundaries can be reduced because you have developed these key processes. And that's the subject of our next chapter.

Step 4: Reduce Your Boundaries

*The Comanche understood such things as truces, border arrangements,
and trading relations, for the tribes and bands worked these out
with each other constantly ... The Spanish insisted upon making
agreements in treaty form with a Comanche nation as Europeans
carried on their relations with each other ... The Spanish and those
who followed them could not understand an organization that did not
go beyond the hunting group ... The war chief's authority to make
a truce normally did not extend beyond a single war party or the
conclusion a single war trail.[10]*

*No treaty ever signed with any tribe upon the plains was ever
completely valid, from this fact alone.[11]*

In order to truly achieve Fluid Form, you will need to reduce, cross, or minimize the boundaries. Perhaps it makes sense to combine two departments in order to reduce the complexity of the work. We have already seen the benefit of combining different processes and initiatives.

Reduce boundaries to reduce complexity—that's the goal. Where possible, reduce the number of departments, functions, processes, or processes-and-initiatives combined. Reducing complexity, while bolstering cross-functional processes will be up to the managers and will show how far you are willing to go to create Fluid Form. It's not like everything has to be a cross-functional project or process, but some of these things really need to be designed more robustly if they are going to be successful. Certainly the more important ones need to be identified and the unnecessary ones eliminated.

---

10 Fehrenbach, *Comanches*, 184-5.
11 Ibid., 371.

Generally, we think of an organization in terms of the organization chart: some sort of hierarchy with major units or departments that are further subdivided into sections at lower levels. This division of labor orchestrates the work required. Try imagining no organization at all. Would everyone do every job? How would the work process steps be completed if there were not some coherent grouping of people based on the types of work required?

Organization charts are the fearful, controlling response to what is speculated as a chaotic environment if a gaggle of people roamed about the work area, picking and choosing whatever each wanted to do.

The question remains how best to make divisions, draw boundaries around sets of activities or steps in the process to create order without artificially creating a boundary that becomes a work process break. All boundaries—where a department box might be drawn—have the great potential of becoming a barrier in the work process. There is no scientific algorithm that can make a "correct" choice.

On the other hand, a boundary could be drawn where there appears to be the least obstruction to the flow of work or where there is a natural completion of a subset of the work. At this point, the efficiency of that sub-process could be measured to provide feedback to those doing the work.

Here's where you get a chance to apply Fluid Form concepts by organizing around process, with the flow of work first. Remember our warehouse filled with Droids! Consider leadership and coordination as functions that could be divided or shared. The challenge here is to *not* create more functional groups or departments (horizontal boundaries) than are really necessary.

There is a tendency to feel comfortable with a firm structure, as opposed to a structure that is more process-based and more likely to change over time. Draw boundaries that help divide the work to reduce complexity and provide coherence for humans while trying not to create what could become barriers to the natural flow of the primary work processes.

It will be challenging, but forget thinking about organizational structure except as a snapshot in time of who is working on what. Give up trying to create a fixed organization. Trust that the organization will be what it needs to be at any point in time. The goal in this part of the process is to redesign and reduce unnecessary boundaries to:

- Reduce complexity
- Link related work
- Determine the level of work that must be managed locally
- Determine the type and level of work that can be managed centrally
- Determine Process/Project Teams for cross-functional construction

Chances are, your organization structure is opportunity-rich for reduced horizontal boundaries, flattened hierarchy, sensible projects/ process linkages, and effective integration for total organization success.

Key questions to consider: How can you reframe "organizational structure" as an array of project teams with changing membership based on area of focus? Where can you reduce or remove functional groupings? Where does it really make sense to draw a boundary?

Let's take a look at a company that was able to remove their shackles and considerably reduce complexity.

Inside Allied Signal

If you worked for the U.S. Department of Energy (DOE) and were in the market for non-nuclear parts for atomic bombs, chances are they came from the Allied Signal plant in Kansas City. As the customer for this type of sensitive product, the DOE managed the facility security, established and regulated the processes for the building, and ensured overall quality. Opportunities to improve the efficiency of the quality assurance program surfaced in the late eighties, and I was hired as a consultant to lend a hand.

In the same breath that they asked for advice, they bragged that they consistently received the "Diamond Seal Award" from DOE for their exceptional quality performance.

While probing into the current process for ensuring this exceptional quality, I couldn't help but find myself in the middle of DOE's mandatory steps requiring seven separate quality reviews before certifying their products. In fact, if I ever had a nanosecond of wavering about following the rules and regulations here, I had vigilant, machine gun-toting security guards around me as a silent reminder.

Layers of checkers checking the checkers had long since been viewed by more modern approaches as being outdated, redundant, more time consuming, costly, and ultimately not as effective. Deming's statistical process controls and the more current practice of building quality into the manufacturing process—rather than relying on a third party after each build to check on quality—were now commonplace. Procter & Gamble, for example, had designed quality responsibilities as part of the operator's role.

It wasn't long before I began to wonder if my assignment in Kansas City was seriously intended to result in change at all, or if it was meant to solidify their view that they had to keep doing it the way they were doing it. After all, DOE was happy with the results, and Allied Signal most certainly had to follow the DOE's established process of multiple checkpoints.

As is often the case in these organizations, there were those who were drawn to, and enjoyed, the process of "policing" the operations and making approvals at each step along the way. Was my role really meant to be a third party validation to DOE that the plant was as efficient in the process of assuring quality as they were in delivering quality products?

To understand the DOE regulations, I went directly to the source: the DOE. Although it had been more research-focused, I'd had some experience with them while working at Lawrence Livermore Laboratory, and I didn't remember anything resembling this antiquated process. Remarkably, my research uncovered that the DOE standards had changed several years earlier in response to Deming's work and the changing trends in quality assurance over the previous decade. In fact, the DOE regulations now seemed drawn from Deming and the latest thinking.

The hallowed "seven steps" not only were no longer required—they didn't even *exist* in the updated guidelines! The Kansas City facility was likely the last bastion of this practice where they were nurtured with a gospel-like adherence to detail. Shackles removed, they were now free to build quality into the operational processes and eliminate the hierarchal intrusions of a separate quality function.

Here is another successful example where two companies were able to reduce a boundary, and turn a customer supplier roadblock into a win-win.

Inside GE and Exxon—Working It Out

After scores of successful Work-Out processes within GE, they decided to push beyond their own walls, to their suppliers. Exxon was a key supplier to GE's Plastics Division. Despite conversations between the head GE buyer and Exxon supplier counterparts to address delivery schedules and cost issues, not much had been resolved. The ongoing frustration at both ends led GE to propose the cross-organization Work-Out. Exxon was ready to try something else to resolve the lingering issues with this important customer.

As with the internal Work-Outs, the people in the trenches dealing with the issues on a daily basis were called in to detail the problems and propose workable solutions that made sense to both parties. As always seems to happen when the front lines meet and problem-solve together, solutions were indeed formulated. At this point, they were presented to the higher-level decision makers—

who hadn't been able to come up with a solution on their own—for review, modification and approval.

The senior executives from both companies had no difficulty in ratifying what was now viewed as a win-win solution—not perfect for either side, but significantly better than the ongoing lose-lose standoff.

In a small way, this illustrates how Fluid Form organizations would likely interact on a regular basis. The movement, changing structure, and enhanced permeability that characterizes Fluid Form would be carried over to an inter-organizational field of Fluid Forms. The array of people, the nature of their involvement, and the intensity and context of their effort, would all change. This reformulation across a common field of interaction seems a far better way to visualize how Fluid Form organizations would interact than through some formal set of rules of engagement or through some formal processes of decision-making that would involve movement and approvals up and down various silos in the hierarchies.

The intelligence that guides the focus and reformation of people and projects is embedded in the field itself, not through hierarchal controls. As one piece moves, the others are aware. Knowledge frozen today in the vertical silos is more broadly shared across these organizations. Next-best moves and actions are easier, because the situation in the field is more extensively understood. Opportunities to make effective choices are more obvious to those involved.

Fluid Form can be applied not just to business problems, but to other pressing situations as well. Consider the following example:

Inside Special Education

A man we'll call Jerry was recovering from a heart attack, advised by his doctor to slow down, reduce his hours at work, and find a way to dampen his daily stress level. Working for the state government as the manager and advisor to all of Oregon's special education programs, he found himself inundated with scores of requests each day to clarify how the new laws affected schools, social workers, and, ultimately, the kids.

The federal government had recently mandated that the goal for special education children should be to mainstream them, which meant moving them into regular classes as soon as possible, even if their disabilities left them at a disadvantage with regular students. The intent was that mainstreaming was more likely to help them become self-sufficient in life than if they were left confined in special education classrooms.

The calls for help from social workers and schools came in faster than Jerry could respond, leaving him frenetic, hounded, and criticized for the state's inability to meet the queries. I arrived as a half-time assistant to field as many of the calls as possible. It didn't take me long to join in on the frustration with the endless stream of queries, which was only exacerbated by the confusing double speak of the new federal law, PL 94142. Even tag-teaming this thing, we still were falling behind. Becoming as harried as Jerry, I talked him into doing an analysis of the calls. We found that eighty percent of them were coming from an adjacent department of Family Services.

Except at the agency head level, crossing into another agency to deal with difficult issues is often seen as inappropriate. In fact, even doing the analysis was a potential feather-ruffler. The hundreds of social workers in the field were not in the school system, but represented individual families who were confused and floundering when their kids were moved out of special education programs and put into regular classes. Their questions were, "Why is this happening?" and "What can you do to help these families?" Angry and bewildered, they felt victimized by a change they believed was unjust.

Eighty supervisors managed the hundreds of social workers. Our response included working directly with them so we could understand their confusion, and then developing a two-day training program that had the answers—basically, a formalized brain dump of Jerry. Within a month, the call level dropped from a flood to a trickle. Relief and genuine appreciation oozed from the social workers and their supervisors in Family Services. We had just put me out of a job!

In fact, we may have done the same for Jerry. His blood pressure went back up for a different reason: he became worried that he didn't have enough to do to justify his full time position. The problem seemed so easily solved once we crossed the line and made the connections. The obvious lesson is that information centralized at the top of a hierarchy prevents effective cross-organization interaction. Jerry had never intended to be the bottleneck, but he was in a different agency than Family Services, and until I arrived he followed the unspoken rule: don't move information and problem-solving down and across organizations to allow for creative and quick solutions.

Fluid Form opens the door for improvement in the following ways:

- More permeable boundaries between organizations and processes invite other interested parties to become creatively engaged at the grass roots level.

- Problems and opportunities are seen from a broader perspective, because more involvement occurs from a wider set of vantage points.

- With fewer barriers about which organizations can be engaged, the field of play is enlarged, and the likelihood for improvement in unforeseen areas is opened up.

- There is greater likelihood that related processes will connect with similar ones, which means that good ideas will be shared more often.

- Broader involvement and more thorough discussion lead to solutions that are more robust, with more support for implementation.

Once Fluid Form teams and relationships are created, it is extremely important to ensure and maintain open boundaries between executives, sponsors, and all team members. Too often, after project process teams are created, lack of communication inhibits productivity. Managing the boundaries between related projects and processes is very important. You want to be aware of whether you're getting the expected results, or if, perhaps, a process or team needs redirection.

My view is that the project and process teams don't have enough of this going on so that they falter and fail. And a major cause of these failures is not having the information technology and robust structure to allow teams to communicate effectively. That's the subject of the next chapter.

Step 5: Create the Virtual Homeroom

Developing Robust Fluid Form Teams

The discipline and organization of the Comanche war parties, measured against the whole tenor of Comanche life and culture, always surprised Europeans. But war was a serious business, and its practice had taught all Indians the value of tight discipline, careful planning, and control.[12]

Comanche warriors were really hunters, stalking their prey. And they retained a full range of hunting skills that had long disappeared in the agrarian world.[13]

No European army marched, or could march, with such wilderness skill, such personal discipline, or for that matter, such implicit deadliness.[14]

If you're going to create robust, cross-functional Fluid Form teams, they need a place to meet. I call that place the "virtual homeroom." In this chapter, we'll discuss how to provide the infrastructure and information system technology to create "places" where your teams can "meet"—no matter how far-flung they may be, across your organization or across the globe.

In today's world, your people are literally all over the map, not just all over the office. If your organization still operates as a hierarchy, many of your members remain inaccessible to other members,

---

12 Fehrenbach, *Comanches*, 72.
13 Ibid., 73.
14 Ibid., 74.

and also to information. Compartmentalized roles may make it challenging for everyone on your team to get on the same page at the same time. If you are attempting to create Fluid Form, then the virtual homeroom is one way to have people come together, even if they cannot physically be in the same room.

The homeroom is a virtual meeting place where people can add to a list and brainstorm at different times. When it is convenient, they may come together and look at the list that has been put together. They spend an hour in the room doing decision-making, based on what they've already done, which reduces the total amount of time taken away from their other work. From the practical point of view, virtual tools are necessary for these projects and processes to be successful, because of the demands on people's time.

Certainly, it's easy to cast the hierarchal system as the major roadblock constraining the success of horizontal teams in their pursuit of performance improvement. I've shared some of my experience, and there's plenty more. A more productive path to unleashing an organization's full potential is concentrating upon creating and maintaining a supportive infrastructure where teams can not only survive, but more importantly, THRIVE.

It's time for a different building block to encourage the evolution of a flatter, more networked organization. This will require a true virtual homeroom with such solid and engaging structure that it more than matches the pulls and demands of its traditional counterpart.

The track record of benefits that Fluid Form teams create will drive the demand for organizations designed with such teams as the basic building block. It is possible, then, that a more Fluid Form of organization—which requires less of the traditional hierarchy—would also achieve the aims initially intended by bringing step function change to organizational effectiveness.

Organizations today are prolific with various forms of project and process teams—but as vehicles aimed at breaking through bureaucracy to accelerate and improve results, the level of success of those teams has been mixed, at best. Organization improvements that were begun with socio-technical systems—and subsequently extended with quality programs and business process re-engineering—have produced exceptional results, but only when these more horizontal approaches were built with sufficient sustaining infrastructure. Cases in point:

- Procter & Gamble built autonomous work teams based on each individual acquiring multiple skills.
- Jack Welch at GE reduced the number of vertical levels and promoted a "boundary-less" approach to support cross-functional collaboration.
- W. L. Gore limited the size of his manufacturing plants to reduce hierarchy, while also building flatter teams.

For most companies, though, the payoff of building organization success through horizontal networks and teams has never come close to realizing its full potential. In fact, when a team is not successful, the damage of its "failure legacy" can be surprisingly far-reaching. The collective sense of wasted time and effort on "just another unnecessary activity" can virtually cripple future efforts or discourage organizations from implementing similar initiatives altogether. Ask any consultant!

The January 21, 2006 issue of the *Economist* included a special section on "The New Organization." It highlighted that the advent of the knowledge worker, replete with all the new communication devices and often operating remotely, has coincided with the proliferation of teams at all levels of the organization. These run the gamut from small projects to new product development teams. The article goes on to claim that these horizontal and ad hoc teams, embedded in vertically-oriented structures, result in more complex work *without* the organization effectiveness intended.

And so, people with a different vision continue to throw seeds on concrete. Trends increasingly seem to lean toward building more types of project and process teams, yet the breakthrough, fertile structure that would make this approach truly successful remains elusive.

Key questions to consider: Do you have distributable, system-wide tools to maintain the focus on the problems at hand, report status and aid in work completion? Are they integrated? Will you "make or buy" such tools? Are you using and knowledgeable about the latest Web 2.0 applications such as social-networking, video sharing, wikis, podcasts and blogs? What do you need to put in place, and by when?

Information and communication overload increases with both old and new technology. I've heard some managers report that their daily emails average as high as six to seven hundred—let me repeat, six to seven HUNDRED! This level probably has increased for each manager gradually over the last four or five years. Like the classic "boiling frog" that is slowly being heated, they have learned to respond to the increased heat each year by hanging in there, taking laptops home (and on vacation!), and cranking out responses in the middle of the night to keep abreast. There's a point where many employees are too scared *not* to respond to their email.

Meanwhile, meetings—the tried-and-true method of resolving differences, solving problems, and keeping everyone on the same page—have not decreased in use. But they still have the reputation for being mostly time-wasters, despite the increase in electronic connections. Columnist John MacIntyre reports on a survey by GroupSystems that showed that during the typical weekly staff meeting (averaging 50 minutes), 56 percent say action items are documented only sometimes or not at all, and 68 percent say input from the discussions is used only sometimes or rarely when implementing action items.[15]

All this inefficiency contributes to time overload, which organizationally creates the inevitable conflict among assignments. While prioritizing has its time management merits, individuals must

---

15 John MacIntyre, "Corporate America Stuck in Meetings," *San Jose Mercury News*, April 2, 2006.

juggle when and how much of which initiative to serve, while at the same time lobbying with others for their time commitment where cooperative efforts are essential. It is common now to play multiple roles, resulting in the endless cross fire of demands where, on any given project, the critical mass of combined effort is not achieved because key players are fighting on different fronts and unavailable to connect in a meaningful timeframe to get work done. Unchecked, the situation can be a bit psychotic.

Information overload is one barrier. When it's combined with the hierarchal performance appraisal system, with its functionally segmented bias, they create an ominous hurdle to the deployment and relative success of cross-functional teams. Without establishing a matrix organization, all the conflicting forces characteristic of it are now rampant in nearly every large organization. There is lots of buzzing about, without enough concerted, meaningful effort in the project teams to achieve their intended purpose. Lots of *activity,* but little meaningful *action.*

For Fluid Form teams to flourish, participation relevance needs to go beyond legislated assignments and the resultant obedience or obliging willingness that typically follows. While those with core or leadership roles may be motivated by surveillance or pressure to achieve results, the other limited-role participants (or "professional hideouts") are most likely to drift away. While building sufficient homeroom infrastructure makes it easier to participate, in terms of being on top of project assignments and progress—as well as less onerous, because of more efficient use of time—effective participation still depends on motivated and enthusiastic engagement. Since this cannot be mandated, it must be constructed as a separate system that supports these behaviors. Indeed it is a handful of separate, yet integrated, systems that is required to provide critical mass for Fluid Form team support.

The "virtual homeroom" sustains the ongoing problem-solving and decision-making that characterizes a Fluid Form team who actually are all in the same room working full-time on one project.

Over time (and most likely with some costly trial and error), most companies have learned to build project team infrastructure sufficient to provide focus, direction and support from one or more managers outside of the team and further up the hierarchy. A typical chartering process includes goals and metrics, key performers and a team leader, representative membership from functions or groups that need to be a part of the solution or have a stake in the outcome, and a sponsor or link to the management team that sparked this initiative. While this architecture appears adequate for most project endeavors, the failure of so many temporary project or ongoing process teams to deliver results in a timely fashion—or to deliver desired results at all, for that matter—suggests that there is a breakdown somewhere.

Scores of teams have solved problems. I know, because I've been in team meetings where we've papered the walls problem-solving to come up with solutions that would never have materialized if we hadn't "locked" ourselves in the same room for a day or more. If you've spent time in a large organization, I trust you have similar stories of your own. What seems to break down is the follow-up. The teams I have been on find it hard to get everyone back together to implement with the same enthusiasm we had when we started.

Some people think that cross-functional, horizontal teams are ill-conceived as an organizational vehicle to produce results. Yet documented cases of exceptional results directly challenge that hypothesis. A more realistic conclusion is that project team infrastructure isn't sufficiently robust to achieve predictable, high-return results. Of course, adequate infrastructure simply does not guarantee effective team operations. You've got to contend with these issues, as well:

- Other responsibilities, priorities or interests that pull individuals away;
- Difficulty convening the team in one place at one time;

- Lack of information about individual work status and projected completion;
- Inability to maintain critical interfaces with related projects or initiatives;
- Unclear overview of achievements and remaining tasks;
- Inability to deal with new issues or changes in the situation;
- Inability to rethink, refocus, and update the plan.

Picture a planning meeting where, one by one, people get cell phone calls or emails and drift out of the room, some not coming back, some drifting back after short or lengthy intervals, their minds clearly on issues other than the meeting at hand. That wasn't hard, now was it? How many times have you planned the myriad other things you're going to do during a meeting—emailing on your Blackberry or surreptitiously reading reports on one side of a notebook while pretending to take notes on the other? Even better is to be suddenly called out for a "must attend to issue," all pre-arranged with a colleague. When all else fails, missing the meeting because you need to "meet a deadline," and then sending an apology later, usually ensures all is forgotten in the fog of busyness everyone else understands.

Sometimes the weariness of too many agendas makes it hard to stay awake. I remember falling asleep and then falling out of my chair at one of those multi-day planning sessions. I couldn't think of an excuse short of narcolepsy, which I felt was a little bit of stretch at the time. They were still laughing at me a week later.

This issue of keeping teams on track is not uncommon today, but the problem can be remedied by designing, agreeing to, and enforcing ground rules like requiring people to turn off their communication devices when everyone is in the same room at the same time. Unfortunately, projects of significance usually have a longer time horizon; work must be accomplished when people are in different places; and tasks that are related are completed at different points in time.

The different ways to drift away and become disconnected are many, and the cumulative effect of the many tugs to focus on other activities devolves into the symptoms listed above. The key to building critical mass lies in developing solutions that overcome the pervasive issue list that confounds project team success.

Inside Intel

When managed care first came on the scene, Intel changed its healthcare system to the newly evolving approach, hoping to achieve significant savings. From the start, problems plagued the new program. There was confusion about how to receive claims, how to process them, and how much insurance covered vs. co-payments. The result was a quagmire of frustration and finger-pointing emanating from CIGNA, the provider—which was also new to the managed care system—to the Intel Benefits group and nearly all the employees accessing this cumbersome system. Feeling like the kids stuck between two battling parents, the Benefits Group was a little scared—for their careers. It got to the point where senior executives weren't using the system, preferring to pay their bills personally rather than take the time to wrestle the back-and-forth negotiations required for reimbursement.

The heat was on. The professional mangers and engineers were furious. When one of the employee's dependents with a life-threatening emergency was sent back and forth between two of the program's hospitals, because neither one accepted the individual as a program participant, the red flag went up. The CEO, Andy Grove, hollered for a swift and immediate overhaul of the program.

Easier said than done. The people in the Benefits Group were the ones who best understood the details and the confusing and obfuscating elements of the managed care process. They were also the ones caught in the current chaos, spending most of their time putting band-aids on hemorrhages, and they were, therefore, unavailable to spend the concentrated time necessary to comprehensively review and overhaul the entire system. Tough choice that is, the frying pan or the fire!

By the time they raised their hand for help, the Group looked like they were spiraling down into a whirlpool. Each adjustment to the system created more problems than it solved. The harder they worked at it, the more frustrating and demoralizing it became. Their attempts to "fix" problems meant that individual issues were solved without thinking through how they impacted other system elements. Not surprisingly, things got worse, as each fix led not to solutions, but to even more dysfunction. Incremental changes led to more monumental problems. Regardless of the staff's day-to-day firefights, continuing without a major redesign that stopped the bleeding (so to speak) was not an option.

The remedy? A more robustly-designed team with all the "right" players who could focus together on the design of a new system without having the burden of trying to meet the daily demands of the present. The right players did include significant participation from the Benefits Group, which was already overstretched, as well as liaisons from Cigna, the provider. Also on the team were IT, and field HR reps and managers/users who had their own ideas about how things should work. I decided that the only way out of this morass was a two-pronged approach: create twin groups, one that kept the existing system running as well as possible, and one that was chartered to design a revamped system that met the expectations of service originally contracted.

With the majority of the Benefits Group participating in both teams, their roles, task sets and time commitments had to be clearly defined. After suggesting they juggle what appeared to be two full-time jobs simultaneously, I earned my share of "skunk eyes" from the staff. They would have to shift between both jobs and be able to don the different hats, first working on the day-to-day issues, and then shifting to their role in designing the new system. In a word, they had to be fluid. This may seem like an obvious and unspectacular idea.

But doing it, and really getting it right so that the time commitment and task expectations were achievable, took careful thought and negotiation.

Roles and time commitments shifted as the project moved forward, requiring periodic readjustment, so the robust infrastructure of the project team could be maintained. Without that rigor, there would be no success in any reasonable timeframe, if at all. The approach did work. A new system was designed that did meet original expectations. Along the way, more complete performance metrics were identified, with improvement targets set for successive years. The two-team design also spawned a similar process for resolving future systemic problems. As a byproduct, Cigna had enhanced their ability to deliver managed care to their other clients.

The basic components required for robust Fluid Form teams today are rooted in the same socio-technical work teams pioneered by companies like Procter and Gamble many decades ago. Team members were expected to adapt to varying workloads, to learn more than one function, and to perform tasks in different ways. They were rewarded for learning and being proficient in new tasks as well as for their creativity, initiative, and teamwork to solve problems and implement solutions.

The issues around participation, ability to problem solve and stay on top of progress in real time and to simulate everyone in the same room working on one project are collectively the issues that must be attained to achieve critical mass.

Project success, time after time, hinges on this capability, which cannot be attained with our outdated stories of adequate infrastructure. This capability must simulate the look and feel of everyone working together in the same room, as if this was their only job, even though they are also engaged with other roles and assignments. This can be achieved with a real-time information system that has the *appeal* of an online game, which fully supports the project team and creates that war room energy and focus as they work together in a virtual reality.

Five Requirements for Constructing Robust Fluid Form Teams:

- Role and Membership Fluidity
- Team Self-Sustainability
- Integrated Problem Solving and Action Planning Tools
- Open Boundaries
- Comprehensive Scorecards or Dashboards

Role and Membership Fluidity

When defining individual roles for Fluid Form teams, the standard set of variables includes:

- Expertise offered
- Specific contribution expected
- Level of involvement (core, support, review)
- Time commitment

Membership fluidity means the ability to accommodate an array of changes in the composition and roles of project participants. The ability of a team to accommodate each of these determines what might be called a fluidity index:

- "On-boarding" new participants and getting them up to speed
- Removing participants for good cause, without prejudice
- Expanding an existing role because of interest or capability
- Reducing the task load because of interest or to balance other assignments
- Changing the composition of the role or exchanging roles
- Adding elements of team coordination or leadership

Ultimately, membership fluidity matches individual interests with the requirements of the team for sufficient talent to complete the job. Just as individuals have preferences relative to their career, so does the Fluid Form team have changing requirements over time, so it will need to shift the player resources in line with the shifting set of tasks required. Obviously, situations where teams must periodically alter focus or work requirements call for a higher degree of membership fluidity. Yet, regardless of the degree of change expected, you need both team infrastructure and member flexibility.

In my own experience, I have resisted being a member of numerous teams because neither my role nor the time commitment were clear to me. Maybe more importantly, changing the nature or level of my contribution was something I did not easily buy into once I got started. Haven't you come up with a litany of reasons not to participate in similar situations for much the same reason, even when you knew this was an important issue that you could help on?

The ability to include participants in remote settings and engage in a significant amount of problem-solving work independently (which reduces total meeting time) does lower resistance to participation, making it easier to recruit and involve the right players. The most frequently heard complaint on project teams is that so much time is wasted in meetings. Indeed, more flexibility and efficiency also means that individuals who might be limited in their involvement in traditional teams may be able to contribute far more in this new scenario—both more in terms of value add as well as energy and enthusiasm.

For those in the latter years of their career or part-timers, there is more chance to become engaged in projects that do not require full-time participation. Membership fluidity also enables an organization to better tap into scarce technical masters. At Procter &Gamble many of the experienced "black belts" have retired and they are having to seamlessly flow the remaining masters across initiatives, projects, and organizations.

Team Self-Sustainability

Managing successful teams can be a delicate balance. The nature of teams means that team membership and role assignments will change over time; the downside is, it may become especially difficult to maintain focus and complete necessary tasks. The exposure escalates further when the team leader moves on and there is a gap in leadership, or a new person arrives who needs time to get up to speed. Building Fluid Form team self-sustainability is essential to constructing support systems that have critical mass. This means diversifying the leadership capability among the team itself, not relying on one person to be the sole owner of coordination and leadership.

As we discussed, a large part of the success for Procter & Gamble's technician systems relied upon the operators' ability (and willingness) to absorb the coordination and leadership roles that were once solely the province of first-line supervisors. Along with that, P&G provided the elbow room for them to set their own goals and make decisions themselves or with others on the work site, without hierarchal approval. The focus and coordination of activities was shared, which provided greater collaboration and backup leadership when needed, whether there was a designated team leader or not. Managing the boundaries with other stakeholders and groups in their process flow was also integral to the shared leadership concept. These fundamental socio-technical concepts are applied and extended in the Fluid Form context.

To achieve this fluidity requires a multi-skill approach, where the dimensions of leadership are assigned or taught to several Fluid Form team members. Along with reducing the risk of a leadership vacuum, involving others in coordination and leadership functions makes better use of resources to meet variations in work demand

and promotes a broader sense of accountability for Fluid Form team results. The set of skills required include the ability to:

- Define key issues
- Prioritize key issues
- Develop solutions
- Agree upon critical actions
- Determine responsibility for assignments and action plans
- Accept accountability for individual assignments
- Rigorously monitor all team project variables
- Maintain critical interface relationships
- Build confidence
- Build energy and momentum

Often, teams that have lost their leader have allocated one or more of these functions and successfully replicated the role of one leader, as illustrated in the *StorServ* example, where the duties were successfully divided among several team members.

Integrated Problem-Solving and Action-Planning Tools

Your teams need places where everyone is working together face-to-face with all the information about their project on screens or wall-sized reports, which is what the virtual information system must simulate. It is simply not enough to communicate via email or in an ongoing series of meetings to recreate any experience that approximates the actual homeroom we're envisioning. In the best of cases, having access to Cisco Systems TelePresence video conferencing capability, for example, allows meeting participants to see the wealth of visual, non-verbal communication that provides the nuances of meaning that are otherwise unavailable.

As outlined earlier, to provide the quality of problem-solving, action-planning and monitoring of tasks and results, the virtual homeroom must have all these standard tools available in an integrated and accessible way. When you enter the homeroom, all the tools and information that are traditionally used when working on a project must be available so the same type of problem-solving a Fluid Form team might use when they are face-to-face can occur in the virtual system. The caveat here is that, like other web-based virtual games, the inputs and responses may not happen in real time, but over some agreed time period, to allow for time zone and location differences.

The homeroom information system must contain a minimum standard set of integrated tools that allow for reasonable customization to the situation at hand just as one would expect to be able to do when everyone is in one room, to support the following activities:

- Surveys—rating scales, multiple choice, open-ended
- Brainstorming—lists, categorized lists, force field analysis
- Decision-Making—ranking against one or more criteria, checklists
- Action-Planning—Responsibilities, deadlines, resources needed
- Progress and Scorecards—Task status, forecasting, results tracking

Only in this way can the more robust Fluid Form team infrastructure required for success be achieved. Indeed, the test for adequate robustness is that whatever ability a Fluid Form team has when they are in the same room is what must be simulated in the virtual homeroom. You're welcome to visit my website, **www.ChangeCompanion.com**, for an introduction to the problem-solving software I created to support the homeroom concept outlined in this chapter.

Excellent solutions often don't get off the table (or whiteboard) and onto implementation because there is no visible tool to keep people aware of what they need to do. The process of getting things done is an iterative cycle that requires adaptation to changing events and results. The community of people engaged in implementation must periodically communicate to evaluate progress and refine or alter plans or direction. Individuals and whole teams waste precious time and energy moving down an unnecessary path when the environment has changed. It is imperative to refocus and realign, to "refresh" the team, just as you would a browser displaying old data.

Implementing requires surveying for new understandings of the situation, brainstorming to develop alternate approaches that reflect new information, and prioritizing to transform good ideas into good decisions and an updated plan. More importantly, being able to recalibrate the situation and reconfigure direction allows for the renewal of purpose and meaningfulness. The tools to do this must be available at all times, not just at periodic meetings.

Fluid Form teams don't have to be able to problem-solve and plan all the time, but they do need this capability far more frequently than they can actually be together. With this robust information system infrastructure, project teams can more easily engage participants, because of its inherently greater operational flexibility.

Open Boundaries

Isolation can be the greatest enemy of Fluid Form team success. Like most others, I tend to slap the blinders on when I am engrossed single-mindedly on a project. Connecting and checking in with other related projects are "naturally occurring" weaknesses. Even though a Fluid Form team may have the latest information, there are other important links that warrant attention. Thinking of the Fluid Form team as having an open boundary, where it can be influenced by other relevant stakeholders, may be viewed as opening the door to unnecessary tampering. In fact, opening and managing boundaries increases support for success. It might be considered "project insurance." It is here that the ability to select and use Web 2.0 technologies (social-networking, video sharing, wikis, podcasts and blogs) in a focused and disciplined way can provide the operational "insurance policy."

Fluid form teams build into the coordination and leadership tasks just this sort of active communication, to maintain links to:

- Sponsors and key executives
- Related initiatives and projects

Knowing as early as possible that the direction, or simply an element of a project, needs to change in some way is the obvious benefit. You need to maintain the right fit with related initiatives. You also need to invite oversight that turns into support, if maintained on a regular basis. Nothing is as disruptive as upset executives who discover, well into a project, that the direction and focus are not to their liking.

Comprehensive Scorecards or Dashboards

Perhaps the most challenging aspect for any project team is to stay focused on the task or project at hand. A rule of thumb is, the fewer objectives, the greater rate of success. Three to five objectives are better than ten or more. These objectives, coupled with appropriate metrics, form the Scorecard or Dashboard that helps prioritize a spectrum of activity. To the extent that these objectives and metrics are defined or fine-tuned by Fluid Form team members, ownership, understanding and commitment help build cohesiveness.

Measurements drive behavior. Scorecards, dashboards, analyzing the data, and constructing an appropriately sensitive monitoring system that generates real time information about progress— without getting mired in excessive detail—are the basis for the other support systems needed. All too often, individual project team participation and performance are neither documented nor factored into the recognition and reward equation. The communication and connections of a specific Fluid Form team to related projects and to key organization initiatives must be visible, to confirm the validity of the project and to close the loop back to rewards for individual participation.

Keeping score has a universal appeal. Keeping track of activity and updating the score are important byproducts of having a scorecard and reinforcing involvement. If it's not clear that you are making headway, then it's easy to lose energy and drift off. I know that when I've been part of a project where my contribution isn't clearly meaningful, I've been "in the room" while my mind has often been somewhere else. For a Fluid Form team, watching the score just as you might read the newspaper headlines each day is the type of visibility that turns a scorecard into an important motivator. The headlines also facilitate keeping important stakeholders up to speed, so that they can intervene in a timely fashion when corrective action can most efficiently be applied, instead of weeks or months later, when it might not only derail earlier efforts but also damage team spirit.

Most importantly, an active scorecard provides a real-time feedback loop to insure that the right work is getting done and that the ball isn't being dropped on one part of the project when it's supposed to connect to another element operating in parallel. It is essential that team scorecards be linked to related initiatives and the high-level enterprise scorecard so when that happens, or when the situation changes suddenly, the headlines appear quickly announcing that action plans must be reconfigured.

The five elements of building robust Fluid Form team infrastructure are far more thorough and complex than typically envisioned— but it's almost always worth the effort. Procter & Gamble has developed a detailed module for virtual teams which parallels these five elements. Sufficient infrastructure allows enterprises like P&G to enjoy the full benefit of horizontal organization. Improved project performance becomes the norm, and Fluid Form capability thus is achieved. For a lot of people, homeroom was the best part of high school. You got to communicate with your buddies and see what was going on before you went off to the specialized classes that made up your day. A virtual homeroom in a Fluid Form enterprise serves the same purpose … and you don't have to scrape the gum off the bottoms of the chairs! In the next chapter you will see how the basic building block of creating virtual homerooms allows you to weave networks and flatten the organization.

Step 6: Assess Coordination Requirements & Weave Networks

Decisions were almost always made by acclamation, when one or more speakers had moved the council. Unless the decision was unanimous, there was none ... Although the council had no means of enforcing its decision, they were always honored and carried out. The problem was that Europeans failed to understand the Comanche's form of society and government. They had no "law" or "government" because they needed none—they were still a people. [16]

The Comanche and the Europeans were never to comprehend one another's laws and government. The Comanche, so far as they understood European arguments, the white men were slaves, always fearful of superiors and bowing to some distant authority, demanding that the red men do the same. [17]

Once you've built your teams and provided them with the information and communications technology they need, it's time to revisit their related work and reassess boundaries. Now, we want to take a look at management to decide how much coordination and leadership are required for each of these teams in terms of these things we looked at in the very beginning: your direction, deployment of projects, allocating and motivating, evaluating, and determining whether you have the right people doing the right things. How can you effectively maintain or manage these teams? Can your team manage itself, or do they need a little encouragement and reinforcement, or maybe some significant direction?

---

16 Fehrenbach, *Comanches*, 45.
17 Ibid., 46.

Many old-school organizations are conceptualized as a management system where departments are defined first, followed by the associated jobs fit into a pre-designed structure—a classic top-down model. Unfortunately, what that model serves is filling slots and balancing the "chart," instead of serving the primary process that is the reason for the organization's very existence.

The levels and progression up and through these structures define the careers that managers aspire to, but they do not necessarily correlate to the amount of management or coordination actually required to support the work. In fact, when the management system is articulated before identifying the critical processes and drawing appropriate boundaries, the artificial boundaries defined by the management system may form barriers to the work processes rather than help coordinate across them.

As the adage goes, managers don't really *do* any real work; their work is in support of primary work processes. There is a grain of truth to that saying, particularly if we think back to the organization staffed only by Droids. Management's role needs an overhaul, and now is your chance to jumpstart that overhaul. There should be no need for operational management beyond what is required to support the coordination of the Droids around the work processes. In the real world, if multi-skill teams can perform much of their own coordination, there is less or no need for immediate supervision, which means less or no need for as many managers to manage the no-longer-needed supervisors.

You've got the chess pieces; now it's time to see how they will move around the board and with what leadership and coordination. It's time to revisit the Breaking Down Boundaries work you completed earlier.

Determine how much and what type of coordination/leadership is required for each project/process team relative to:

- Setting overall direction and developing strategy
- Deploying projects, initiatives, processes, and the teams associated with them

- Allocating human and financial capital to specific parts of the organization
- Motivating, harnessing, and focusing energy and enthusiasm
- Evaluating individual performance and providing feedback for improvement
- Determining where an individual stands relative to meritorious compensation

Who are the stakeholders that should be involved in decision making for each:

- Project/Process?
- Linked Set?

The key questions at this juncture is: *Can these specified decision-making networks provide the required coordination and leadership, or is a single "manager in charge" required? Can fewer managers cover more process and functional areas, because of greater intra-project capability?*

Designing the management structure secondarily allows more of the coordination to be built into Fluid Form teams at a point in geography and time that is closer to the work. This more fully supports effectively managing work processes versus managing people doing jobs, and it supports faster and more accurate decision-making to optimize around the work process. The key question should be "Why?" Why should there be a manager in any given position, and why can't their responsibilities be accomplished by the people closer to the work?

One answer to "why" is when a manager has a level of knowledge and experience to help solve problems, envision a possible path, or determine direction, especially when the situation is unclear. But this question of "why" is rarely asked, because we are used to creating management jobs where we feel there needs to be accountability and one point of control, instead of thinking about building most of these tasks into the teams.

Not assigning a management role creates the fear that there will be a loss of control, with no one to insure that the job gets done. Overcoming this fear and the inertia of relying on one person to keep all the pieces together and focused is the challenge of this phase.

What is the minimum number of managers and hierarchal levels required to insure coordination, leadership, best decisions made? After all, "they're just overhead." Instead of appointing leaders, establish coordination/leadership networks that will supplant unnecessary management and support linked arrays of Fluid Form teams.

Remember to test your choices against the key Fluid Form elements:

- Organize around process, with the flow of work first. Think about it as if you had a warehouse of Droids.

- Consider leadership and coordination as functions that could be divided or shared.

- Consider management as an array of networks with changing membership based on the area of focus.

- Forget about organizational structure, except to think of it as a snapshot in time of who is working on what.

- Forget trying to create a fixed organization. The organization will be what it needs to be at any point in time

Inside Cisco Systems

Ron Ricci, Vice President of Corporate Positioning, outlines the astonishing transformation at Cisco that started in year 2000. Moving away from command and control, CEO John Chambers has created a virtual organization of executive level, cross-functional councils which spawn initiatives (priorities in Cisco terms) that drive business results. They characterize their version of Fluid Form as developing "speed and scale" or more simply, *doing more with fewer resources.*

Councils generally have two or three leaders which include at least two from either operations, sales, engineering, or services. They work collaboratively with other members recruited across the organization. While this may look like a matrix, it is not. This virtual organization is where major business decisions are made. In fiscal year 2007 there were 100 executives involved in 100 priorities; in 2008, 500 executives engaged in 20 priorities and in 2009, 600 executives (headed to 1000) working on 26 priorities.

Who initiates a priority? Could be anyone with an idea that must pass a rigorous test for business viability. As an example the corporate treasurer recently took one of the leadership roles for a priority to build a network business model for sports stadiums. The "to be built" Yankee Stadium is one of the first customers in this newly created market. Clearly being a leader at Cisco isn't just one job anymore. The best and the brightest are engaged on several fronts while playing different roles in each.

What are the results? In 2003 Cisco had 6% of the business phone market. In 2008 their share increased to 25%, a huge gain which they attribute to this evolving Fluid Form organization. To measure "doing more with fewer resources," they highlight that operating expenses as a percentage of total revenue dropped from 38% in fiscal year 2000 to 36% in year 2008 while revenue increased from $18.9 to $39.5 billion. This more effective and continually evolving organization is delivering.

Building decision-making networks and robust Fluid Form teams as achieved at Cisco sets the stage for the mightiest challenge of all—Trim the Pyramid! How much? How far? How much/how little management do you really need to make your organization flow? Can you leap into the abyss and let the networks work?

After you determined your functional initiatives and created your processes, you developed teams in synergy with certain projects. Now you want to take a look at the individual members and determine if networks can manage teams, or if a manager is necessary.

Not all members are at the same level. They're not necessarily all managers or executives. There might be an individual contributor who has tremendous amount of knowledge about a product or a technology, who should be part of that. These are the ones who need to have some kind of oversight to make sure that the project is on the right track, that the right people are involved, and that the project is linked with others and is working in the right direction to get to the goals.

Can these decision-making networks provide the required coordination and leadership? Or does there need to be a manager in charge? Maybe you need a manager, but you have to ask first whether this decision-making group can get by on its own.

"The least management required" means we often don't need a manager. It means that we don't need someone controlling something who is further away from the knowledge of what's actually going on. You trust that the folks in the network to make the best decisions possible about how these projects are going and what they need to be successful, or how they need to be redirected.

It's your job to establish coordination leadership networks that support the various teams. There may be a network that handles several projects because they are related. Maybe there have to be individuals who are part of a specific set of stakeholders, and they need to be part of the project. At this stage, it doesn't matter whether they're called managers or executives or individual contributors— just make sure you have the right people for the job.

Once you weave the network, then you can go back and say, "Do we need this many managers here? Do we really need that anymore?" It's not a question of taking someone out of a job. It's going be more obvious that you don't necessarily need that person in that spot. And in fact, if you leave that person there, they may become an obstruction, because they're trying to control something that they really aren't in the best position to control anymore.

The network's got the right people, they have better information, they're closer to it, and they're going to be able to make better decisions than some managers. It's not just about removing managers to reduce costs—you should not remove managers until you are ready to take them out. It's an evolution, not a revolution here.

Build from the bottom up. You're looking at both management positions as well as levels of management. And in this case, maybe you can take out a level or two of management on the first run, simply because you've built the teams and processes, and you've built the networks that can lead, coordinate, and manage them. Therefore, it becomes obvious that a certain level is no longer necessary.

You will undoubtedly encounter challenges among your members whose individual functions begin to change and grow. Help them see the benefits of these changes. Your members will begin to see the variety of roles that open up to them—a leader here, a player here, a champion over there. Their roles will expand in ways that are will enhance people's view of who they are and what they can do in the organization. The job will become far more interesting, because more opportunities for success will open up. The new plan opens up a career path and makes the job much more open-ended and, in many ways, more entrepreneurial and free-moving than working in kind of a staid, hierarchical organization.

I harken back to the decision-making teams in the General Electric Work-Out example. Most of those team members, at the time, tended to be executives. In many cases, there are other people who have knowledge of the situation. The right people for the job are those who have some stake in what happens as a result of the process. They don't have to have a special title or hold a specific position. If they will be affected as a result of the team's work, then they should be involved in maintaining the team.

Can fewer managers cover more processes in functional areas? Do you have intra-project capability? How many managers do you really need? Now that you have created decision-making networks, what is the minimum number of hierarchical levels required to insure coordination, leadership and best decisions? Remember, Procter & Gamble successfully eliminated the first level of supervision because their teams were capable of their own management. In one plant they eliminated two levels of supervision. So there were only two levels of management in the entire plant: the plant manager and the next level management team. The teams themselves did all the rest, and they did a lot of cross-team coordination.

As we've discussed, Jack Welch went in and took out a layer of management so that, in a division, the top person would have eighteen or twenty reports instead of five or six. He knew that micromanaging is unsuccessful and unappealing—no one really likes to be micromanaged. The manager who now had three times as many direct reports did not have the time to micromanage. He had to manage across boundaries.

The problem with removing a level is that you have the same work for a fewer number of people to do, and it doesn't always mean that it's going to make the organization more effective. If you take a management layer out, you need to build networks that can successfully handle the coordination and guidance required.

The whole approach to Fluid Form is to build teams to do the work. Your teams have to be robust enough to network and in essence they will become their own management. Teams can link across functions and help make decisions and guide processes through networking. Your teams may work better than management, because more of the right people remain involved directly with the work.

When you eliminate levels of management, you will find that your members will rise to the opportunities to effectively govern themselves. I would argue that you create more chiefs in the networks and on the teams, because members learn to develop coordination leadership skills and to share those skills. This is extremely beneficial for your company. You create new leaders and encourage growth and productivity.

It has happened in organizations at Procter & Gamble and other places. Could your organization get too lean? Definitely. But top management is consistently trying to get rid of expensive managers that they don't need. The goal is to not have redundant managers.

Inside Shell Oil

My experience at Shell represents an embryonic example of Fluid Form at work. The particular Shell refinery where I served as a consultant had evolved into a feudal bureaucracy—too many vertical levels, supervisors on top of supervisors. Each of the functional operating units had been entrenched in its area for decades, hiring and promoting from within each unit as if it were a family-run business. People didn't cross the line into another unit, even if the job was the same. As with all heavily functional organizations, every problem was considered the fault of someone else. Operations blamed maintenance for not responding quickly to problems, and maintenance blamed operations for not knowing how to use the system.

Having worked in two other refineries, my consulting team knew the terrain and the typical issues. This refinery was over the edge in terms of its heavily skewed orientation to doing things the same old way vs. responding to business needs. Our challenge was to lean out the organization, build processes and relationships across functions, break up the "family-owned" operating units, and reduce the supervisory and management hierarchy.

With unions in place and a long history of maintaining the status quo, the operators gave us no chance for success. I remember the gleeful expressions on the employees' faces. Underneath was the message that we were nothing if not the latest victims. Plenty of other consultants had walked this turf over the years, only to be chewed up and spit out. They were awfully convincing.

We took our time, delivering significant amounts of education about self-managed teams and the value of processes vs. functional isolation. Without preaching, we hosted scores of field trips to other plants where these systems worked. We enlisted their counterparts at those plants to convey what it was like to make the change from a traditional system. The enrollment continued by involving those same people in a redesign effort. We not only put processes in place, but also broke down the operating units. With boundaries redrawn, people moved. Even after reducing the number of vertical levels, the refinery was still a long way from a project-based, network managed organization. But it was closer, and it worked better.

Imagine how your organization might be redesigned in this direction. Borrow from the Droid analogy and envision how people might cluster around projects or initiatives. You would be part of several projects or teams that had different orientations and your role in each of these might be different. In some, you might play a pure "doing" role, while in other projects, your role might involve more coordination or leadership. These clusters would change composition as the right people moved in and out, based on need. Projects might have short- or long-term life spans, and you might move into teams that were either nearing completion or just starting up. Your role on a project might change over the course of the project. Organization-wide networks that had sufficiently broad collective knowledge would provide focus and direction. Allocation of resources would be determined through dialogue and discussion across networks.

The Decision Making Teams that supported GE's Work-Out process are precursors to just this kind of network oversight. While the more formalized process of Work-Out included any stakeholder group that might be affected by proposed action plans, the networks conceptualized in Fluid Form have both a "push and pull" dimension. More open information systems can be accessed to determine overlaps and interrelationships where coordination may be required. Project Teams will be more effectively influenced by this systemic view of their direction and activity, because they get more comprehensive information from a broader set of stakeholders than they would from a single, "responsible" manager—or even a formalized Decision Making Team.

Linking to related projects, trading, sharing, or reformulating the mix of team players can be accomplished as standard practice in a Fluid Form system, because of the open and connected boundaries between teams. This capability also leads to understanding how the pieces interact to produce organizational performance. Knowledge of how other teams are impacted increases knowledge of how all the projects fit together. As a result, more people have access to the broader perspective once reserved for higher-level executives. When this occurs, focus and direction can come from a flatter organization, because this knowledge exists more broadly—not just at select levels in a hierarchy.

Would you require a hierarchy with even minimal levels to run this organization? If so, what would that look like? Would it be needed to focus on the work that must be done? What would the hierarchy do to make the organization more efficient or effective, if much of the coordination happened across networks? And how would you depict this organization? Certainly not with a standard organization chart, because the composition and lifespan of project teams and networks changes over time—it's not a static model. It is indeed a Fluid Form, because it does evolve, just as any organism changes over time: adapting to its environment, countering threats, and seizing opportunities.

Within organizations, the possibilities of moving toward Fluid Form are apparent. But what about the dynamics between organizations? Today senior members of hierarchies are the gatekeepers deciding who can contact whom between organizations, as well as what specific issues they can discuss. Whether they choose to be the sole point of interaction or selectively delegate someone in the chain of command, they limit those who can dialogue and make decisions. Their isolation and distance from the people directly involved in a specific process or issue precludes the problem-solving, speed and creativity that can occur when those closest to the work are involved. Of course, not every flat organization is a fluid organization, as the following case history relates.

Inside the Unitarian Church

One of my most unusual but interesting consulting projects was with the Unitarian Church. For several years, along with a very charismatic minister, I had developed and taught a series of workshops that combined leadership training with church theology and practice for the many lay leaders who helped organize and often conducted the religious services. The recipe for their cultural stew included liberal social action with protestant tradition plus a sprinkle of Zen Buddhism and an appreciation of other world religions. Despite their openness to different religious perspectives, their world view was not particularly open to anyone who did not share their own. It could be described as a narrow suit of clothes to try to wear comfortably.

Truth be told, I liked their rebellious edge—it smacked of the spirit behind that famous bumper sticker, "Question Authority." They harbored an undercurrent of distrust of hierarchy or organization that might emit the smallest trace of infringing on individual rights or of oppressing any disadvantaged group. Though I was only working in the Pacific Northwest, my understanding from this regional network of ministers and lay leaders was that the "centralized" organization was as flat as any could be, a network of regions that managed collaboratively with little or no hierarchy at all. This certainly didn't surprise me, given their emphasis on autonomy. Still, how they made this work was a head-scratcher that stimulated my curiosity.

The opening came to me one day as an invitation to help this mysterious entity with long-range planning; I dare say, I was excited at this surprise chance to see this array of networks in action. One of the church's main concerns was that they were small compared to other well-known denominations, and their congregation was not growing. Their openness to other religions also opened the issue of identity, education programs, and worship.

We met at a Massachusetts coastal retreat with fifty or so church members, mostly ministers who were charged with leading the rest. Cautiously welcomed, my presence seemed somehow dissonant, as if I were not really in tune, not someone who could be trusted on the inside. This reception wasn't entirely new; I had stumbled into this predicament in previous regional workshops when my choice of language was deemed too business-oriented. Terms like management, metrics, or performance triggered uneasy reactions, a reminder about where I was and with whom I was working. This time, with the focus labeled long-range planning, I felt some comfort that the emphasis was more clearly task-oriented.

Given the environment, I felt comfortable using several standard planning steps, such as reviewing purpose and scanning major issues while pressing for goals with measures. At least one of us was comfortable! But then it all began to unravel. I was quickly reminded that the church already had standing committees that owned the various issues on the table. My seemingly gentle pressure to turn issues into solutions and actions came back at me like a boomerang, a brazen intrusion of business practices. I had done it again—this view had no place in their world. Conceding that I had accomplished little short of irritating them, they persuaded me to do what they could have done without me: break into their ongoing, issue-protective committees.

Reluctantly, I crossed over into what turned out to be the secret of their organization, the power source of the whole shebang. While each committee had assigned members and a focus, I had not known about the most central of all the committees, the centerpiece of this flat, networked organization. It was the "Committee on Committees." Its sole function was to name committees and assign members to them—a most unusual form of control, though it was clearly not the lightning rod of coordination.

They acted as if they had the authority of a high level executive team, but they did not plan, set direction, or promulgate initiatives. There was no adjudication of differences, no identification and prioritization of issues, no intervention into the workings of the other committees. To the most casual of observers, it seemed this organization was, by design, hosting endless conversations about issues without ever taking action: in essence, an endless do-loop of discussion.

Suddenly it hit me that I had been nullified by bureaucracy. The ironic parallel between this flat organization and the most rigid of bureaucracies came down on me like a ton of bricks. At the rudimentary level, it was just as hard to get something done in the "flatland." Its networked and non-hierarchal nature did not inoculate it from the trappings of any other large bureaucracy, where making something happen is an uphill ordeal fraught with quagmires and false turns. What looked like an elegantly coordinated, non-hierarchal network was, in practice, a model of inefficiency, an exquisitely designed "flat bureaucracy." My head-scratcher became a head-slapper.

Once again, they had put to the test and proved that a "business" planner has no place in their domain. It was difficult not to think this was their subconscious way of confirming to themselves that conversation *about* what to do is a more elegant way of being in community than the actual *doing* itself. As I licked my superficial wounds, my guess is that was the lesson. They made a choice by how they organized. This is not a criticism of Unitarian leadership or this deeply thoughtful and caring community. But no wonder there is a fear of networks or shared leadership usurping the known domain of traditional management. There is a real risk that nothing will get done.

In the *Economist* article on the New Organization, the authors note a study reporting that 38 percent of British managers in flatter organizations saw this structure as a barrier to their career. They were tempted to move to another organization that had more rungs on the ladder! This clearly highlights the very human dimension of wanting to be successful, when success historically has been measured by moving up the hierarchy.

Not surprisingly, the socio-technical systems were aimed at optimizing the technical and the social system. The premise is that the way work is organized should factor in both workflow efficiency and human needs for community and job fulfillment. As a result, the job reductionism characterized by the early automated industries was replaced with multi-skill job design, where repetitive single jobs were eliminated in favor of teams where individuals learned and performed a wider array of tasks. This was more satisfying in terms of variety and also provided a progression in achievement based on learning more tasks and taking on more responsibility.

To some extent, this more lateral progression supplanted the progression of moving up the hierarchy. At some point, though, the availability of new tasks to learn is capped by the hierarchal management system, and the "growing" stops. Remember, what was good for the goose *wasn't necessarily* so good for the gander in Iowa City until their very viability was on the line.

The jury is still out whether humans require vertical ascendancy to find true job satisfaction or whether the need to climb is just a byproduct of peer pressure because "everybody's doing it." Minimalize, or eliminate, the ladder—and what happens? Return to the day you walked into a Fluid Form organization and received your assignments—what would be fulfilling and/or missing for you? It's common knowledge that non-Droid organizational life addresses more than one category of needs. The Million Dollar Question is: Can those needs be met without the hierarchal ladder to climb?

Consider a different hierarchy: Maslow's hierarchy of needs in the work context:

- Surviving with enough income to maintain a desired living standard

- Working with a community of people and the quality of those interactions
- Receiving recognition for achievement
- Finding meaning and challenge in the work itself[18]

Now, let's map Fluid Form to Maslow and see how it holds up…

Surviving with enough income to maintain a desired living standard

Let's start with an assumption: in Fluid Form, the survival/income issue is not significantly different from your previous, traditional life.

Support and enjoyment of working with a community of people

I don't think it's a stretch to agree that working in more and varied projects in a Fluid Form organization would enhance this possibility. Ask chronic job-hunters in traditional organizations and assess the likelihood of, and satisfaction derived from, feeling stuck in an unfulfilling situation. Fluid Form offers more opportunities to find better roles and experiences—or at least, to have a balance of good and not-so-good—that is more palatable than the potential isolation in one stagnant slot.

Receiving recognition for achievement

As the *Economist* article suggests, people still overwhelmingly equate recognition with "climbing the ladder"—the big carrot of hierarchal systems. Consider, however, that other forms of recognition might sufficiently supplant this virtually unchallenged concept of success as only vertical success. Examples are out there right now. Architects, attorneys, and doctors value peer and client approval

---

18 Abraham Maslow, *Toward a Psychology of Being* (New York: John Wiley & Sons, 1968).

as much as, or more than, they value moving into management. Journalists rarely move up the ladder, but are rewarded by peers for literary achievement and by ultimately being given the freedom to write on subjects of their own choosing.

In Fluid Form, too, successful work would be rewarded, through team and organization recognition, which would also likely lead to project roles with broader responsibility or challenge. Further, there is nothing in the Fluid Form concept to preclude financial rewards that coincide with effective participation on one of more efforts. Paths more focused on technical specialization, or coordination and leadership, or some mix of both, could more easily find a welcome home in Fluid Form than in traditional organizations.

Finding meaning and challenge in the work itself

There are simply more ways to be engaged in Fluid Form, and a greater variety of challenges available as projects end, as new ones start, and as employees' proven capabilities, as they participate and learn, pave the way for assignments that more closely match their interests. Broader arrays of opportunities further increase the likelihood of not getting stuck in a dead-end job, which means more chances to learn new skills and find work that is meaningful. While no pure Fluid Form exists today, there are legions of networked project structures that have many Fluid Form attributes.

Sometimes, my clients ask whether it's really possible to abandon the traditional notions of hierarchy. How, they ask, do these projects get conceived? Who monitors them, nurtures them or puts poor-performing ones out of their misery? Who assigns people to various projects and makes sure that individuals are neither over- nor under-loaded? How is this monster controlled? These are good questions, since there are few examples to look at where there is no hierarchy managing work. And perhaps there are managing levels of partners that do have power, and that do the work that does answer these questions.

On the other hand, perhaps these same "upper level" folks do this as one of their many roles, as well as participating in other working projects. Perhaps less hierarchal control is actually needed than you think.

Learning theorist Peter Senge and colleagues challenge the notion that hierarchal leadership can be effective in a world of global institutional networks.[19] Instead of depending upon a traditional leader or extraordinary individual, they say, leadership will shift to more distributed, shared networks. While their thinking may not be readily accepted in today's world, pause long enough to examine the possibility. Consider that networks of people who come together with similar intention can experience synchronicity—coincidence of two or more events that seem to occur beyond just a chance happening.

Wall Street Journal columnist, Carl Bialik questions the notion that there are an average of six degrees of separation between any pair of individuals in the world. In a study of Microsoft's instant-message traffic in June 2006, researchers showed that the average number of people needed to bridge any pair of users was 6.6. In a networked organization with open boundaries, the degrees of separation are likely to be even smaller.[20]

In this context, the network and their purpose seem to draw other like-minded people to them. The need for the amount and kind of leadership emerges in the form of the right individuals at the right time—Fluid Form. The staffing of these collaborative networks by an upper-level management team may be unnecessary, if the teams convene more naturally, as projects draw the needed people to them. With a more informed and connected organizational playing field, this is certainly not implausible.

---

19 Peter Senge et al., *Presence: Human Purpose and the Field of the Future* (Cambridge, MA: 2004).
20 Carl Bialik, "We're Far Removed From Proof of Six Degrees Theory," *Wall Street Journal*, August 6, 2008.

If Fluid Form is truly to succeed, then the reward and compensation structure in your organization must evolve along with the changes in work. How to transform the reward scheme is the subject of our next chapter.

Step 7: Evaluate Reward and Progression Systems

Theoretically, all honors and spoils fell exclusively to the war chief, but in practice, every successful war chief awarded honors freely and gave away most of the captured booty.[21]

A warrior who prevented the capture or mutilation of a comrade gained special honor, and any warrior who actually landed a blow by hand, or touch a living enemy, won the highest war honor of all.[22]

As your organization becomes more fluid, the reward scheme must reflect new responsibilities and new tasks.

Are you rewarding people for multiple projects? Are you making it clear that initiatives and projects are just as important as being in a functional group, and is that part of your performance system? If so, then it's going to be easier to move into a longer-term organization where there are fewer management levels. People will see that the things that they do, the people they work with, and the importance of the projects that they're on, will determine their success in the organization. It's no longer about simply moving up the hierarchy. Success becomes a multi-dimensional kind of thing. And it starts off with making sure that there's visibility in terms of projects they work on and who's assessing them, and there's a process in place to make that happen.

Individual Rewards

In a best case scenario, individual effort on a project is also reflected on an individual scorecard. If this is determined by other

---

21 Fehrenbach, *Comanches*, 72.
22 Ibid., 75.

Fluid Form team members, peer pressure to participate positively further supports individual contribution and attention. And, as mentioned earlier, if individual project participation is appropriately weighted with other work, the organizational reward system achieves full integration and support of project teams.

People who feel rewarded for their efforts (either intrinsically or extrinsically) are obviously inclined to work with more enthusiasm. Differences between individuals and generations means rewards can be vastly different. While moving up the hierarchy is for some the answer, finding interesting tasks, working with similarly exciting colleagues, or learning new marketable skills may be the ticket for a younger generation who are not eager to work in a traditionally-structured environment. Membership flexibility on Fluid Form teams creates new opportunities. These opportunities can support diverse reward preferences to the extent that project work is considered in performance appraisal and career development.

Organizations that are extremely functional and hierarchal in orientation may not fully integrate cross-functional assignments. Full support of Fluid Form team success includes the ability of an organization to integrate all the work of an individual, functional and multi-project, and to weight and measure this array of assignments so that it is seen as a fair representation of total effort. Developing Fluid Form capability requires this support be prolific, organization-wide. This is particularly true for a new generation who feels little loyalty to any organization but finds gratification through the specific experience of their assignments and the set of colleagues they are working with at any point in time. Ironically, recognizing achievement and providing opportunities in this context does provide a certain operational loyalty for the time it is available.

Young Gen X and Gen Yrs entering the workforce today should readily embrace the concept of Fluid Form with the right coaching and support from their leadership. From an early age they have lived in a networked world using technology to rapidly connect with friends and family. Unfortunately many of the schools they received their education in were more traditional in nature and encouraged them to narrow their focus into a particular discipline like finance or marketing. Larry Heasley, Manager Human Resources at Shell—Deer Park Refinery, reflects on how this plays out in their refineries. "We find that many of our young engineers in cross-functional production teams are reluctant to compromise their engineering perspective with operations for the overall benefit of the business."

According to Keith Lawrence, a senior HR executive at Procter & Gamble, "the key is helping them confirm their personal strengths and how to put them in play at work. Once they are clear on this they can leverage their unique capabilities in many different situations. Having the opportunity to work more seamlessly across multiple teams and organizations is viewed positively as a way to accelerate their development and have a lot of fun in the process." Similar coaching can also help senior employees who have pigeon-holed themselves in functional roles revitalize their enthusiasm with new work challenges.

How will you reward employees? Perhaps the reward will be monetary—an increase in pay or a bonus. Perhaps changing the nature of the job, or creating multiple roles or new challenges is the reward. If you operate in a hierarchy, or pseudo-hierarchy, move him or her up the line. Provide new leadership opportunities if you operate in a Fluid Form organization as opposed to a hierarchy. If success in the organization is viewed as moving up to the new level, regardless of the project or processes you're involved in, that's not really a Fluid Form concept—because, in the Fluid Form concept, the most successful people are people who take on different roles and can do multiple tasks, and they are rewarded for their overall capability and contribution to the organization.

The most successful employees should also be rewarded from a financial point of view. They should receive more money, and they should have more opportunities that have more importance attached to them down the road. You want to build an organization where people are rewarded for being on projects and processes—where they're filling roles and assignments that move the business and the organization ahead, not just working within a function and trying to work their way up the organization.

Make sure you consider all these roles in the evaluation process. Rewards should not be tied only to seniority. And, in fact, more people should be involved in the evaluation: peers and stakeholders and the networks that have a real view of what the person is doing should have input, as opposed to the evaluation coming from one individual who is a step above in the hierarchy.

It's a Catch-22—the more hierarchy there is, the more likely the measurement system is going to be that way. The further you move toward Fluid Form and projects and networks managing them, the more it's going to make sense for that broader array of people to do the evaluation. Members will be more likely to see their career success as playing multiple roles across the organization, as opposed to being in one job and making one boss happy.

Inside Philips Semiconductor

I once worked for a subsidiary of Philips Semiconductor called Signetics. There, I experienced the limitations of a matrix design. It was possible in the Philips matrix configuration to "report" to a score of managers hovering above from an array of functional entities, while at the same time having a score of lower level managers "report up." While the intent was to make sure that the right people were involved in decisions that might affect them, the net result was that any initiative could be stalled or derailed by one or more of the many constituencies to whom managers were required to report. I'm exhausted just writing about it. Matrix at Philips meant subservience to multiple masters, which involved a considerable expense of energy and time. The paper trail was a sticky spider web of obstacles to getting work accomplished.

What makes this experience all the more difficult is the tug-of-war of the hierarchy—one directed down and across, the other focused up. First to weigh in is the boss's preference for where you should work. Next is your own assessment of the relative priority of the functional and horizontal task requirements, which has to be weighed against which concentration will most impact that vertical element of your career success. In the Philips matrix, the path to success often selected by career managers was to play one "boss" against the "others" in a game of circular mediation that often resulted in nothing happening. Finding the least volatile path of action (sometimes inaction) through the maze, while successfully not rocking anyone's boat, often proved most beneficial to one's career.

While the Philips matrix overstates today's more typical conflict between satisfying the functional demands of your boss versus participating in equally important, cross-functional projects, the prevailing performance review process still emulates management by objectives (MBO), a top-down functional rating of individual performance. Actual work in organizations today does indeed involve functionally channeled work, but much of the work that does make a difference in overall enterprise performance is dependent on a wide array of project teams, which are most typically cross-functional. The hammer-down MBO method is so biased by its vertical lens that meaningful support and encouragement—not to mention real rewards—fail to reinforce the horizontal infrastructure essential for the sustenance of these project teams.

More importantly, hierarchy and its built-in functional focus lead to the disarray and dismemberment of all these efforts initially deemed essential for organizational effectiveness. The ultimate irony is that organizations have evolved to the point where project teams increasingly are being created based on recognizable need, yet the organization spawning them is, in fact, eroding and limiting their potential. Were they to be more adequately supported and nurtured, the concept of Fluid Form organization might well exist more broadly and successfully today. This hierarchal agenda, coupled with the crossfire of too much information and not enough time, is just the recipe to stunt the evolution to a new organizational paradigm.

If you're a military movie buff or grew up in a service family, you're likely familiar with their term for hierarchy: "chain of command." The connotations of "chain" are double-edged. It can mean linked or joined together (connected) and it can mean anything that binds or restrains (shackled). Granted, hierarchy does provide a structure that connects and links, but its strength vertically becomes a shackle when applied to horizontal processes. Therein lies the rub. A well-known personality profile bases its assessment on the notion that an individual's strength, when used in excess, becomes a weakness. Could this be a fair metaphor for what happens in organizations? As more difficulties arise, the hierarchy exerts more pressure that, in this excessive use, only exacerbates the very problems it is attempting to address.

As a former Marine Rifle Platoon Commander in Vietnam, I learned firsthand that hierarchal control was of little value in the midst of a firefight. When the "storm" was coming down in the battlefield, there were times when it was impossible to see, much less communicate with, my Marines only a few yards away. Instead, we individually and collectively relied upon our training and capability to make decisions from where we were and our assessment at the time. Even back then, I began to question why, as officers, we needed to revert so readily back to the rigidity of command and control when a more loosely coupled configuration proved more effective in combat.

Why do organizations reinforce behaviors that support hierarchies? Consider this study, compiled nearly three decades ago across several organizations, which shows that the flow of work and the optimization of efficiencies are not always parallel with career success. The study analyzed various management behaviors across two dimensions. The first explored what management behaviors made the manager's team either more or less effective. The second dimension examined what behaviors made the manager's career more or less successful.

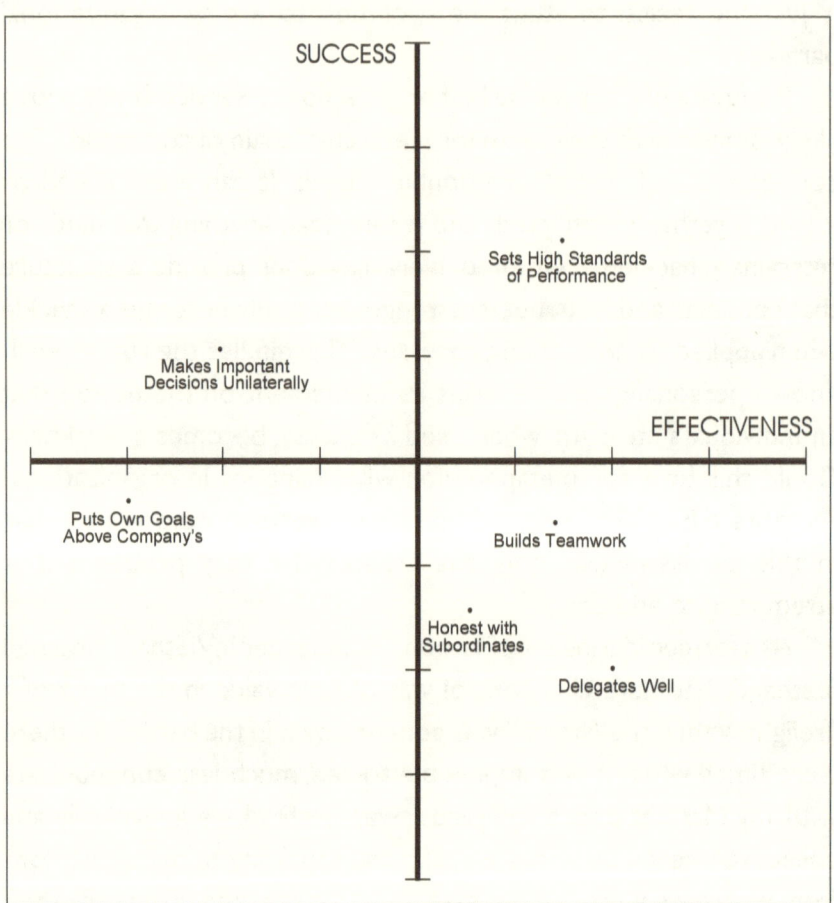

As you can see, setting high standards of performance both enhanced team effectiveness and the manager's career. On the other hand, making important decisions unilaterally had a negative impact on team effectiveness but, surprisingly, impacted the manager's career positively. More interesting (or frightening) was how honesty with subordinates, delegating well and building teamwork—while all impacting team performance positively—had a negative impact on the manager's career.[23]

---

23 Peter J. Graves, *Success Effectiveness Chart* (California State University, San Bernardino, 1979).

Clearly, not all organizations function this way today. But all too often, managers are forced to choose between doing a job the right way and protecting their own upward career path. An example arose at several manufacturing plants I was consulting with in the late seventies. We wanted to know whether creating diversity led to rewards for managers. We discovered that managers conscientiously building diversity into their groups *did* create more effective teams—but their careers were not impacted in either direction. The lesson at that time: doing the right thing relative to diversity was not worth the effort if career success was your main objective.

So in the context of creating reward systems that support Fluid Form, you would want to see something like "performs multiple roles on numerous project and process teams" in the top right quadrant of the matrix above. In other words, reward people who take on multiple roles, so they see clearly how this contributes to success in their own careers. At Cisco Systems, the bonus for everyone is based on total company performance. They are adamant that this is the only fair and effective way to encourage individuals to take on new roles in a dynamic and fluid workplace.

Let me stop and ask you this: How does Fluid Form feel to you now? Can you see yourself in this more dynamic work situation? Can you visualize the kind of assignments you might get, how your weeks and days would look, how you would parse your time between projects, and what new and different projects or roles you might want to experience that could be part of your future? How are your needs being met in this world, and how are they not being met? Do you miss hierarchy, or do you want to stay in Fluid Form? The answers to these questions can help you and your organization move forward on the Fluid Form continuum.

The final issue with regard to rewards is the question of 360-degree reviews—multisource feedback that comes from subordinates, peers, managers and sometimes customers or suppliers. When you've got multiple work situations in Fluid Form, you may need more than one 360-review process because an individual may be playing roles on teams in very different networks. The key is to keep the number of 360-degrees from getting out of hand. Leave the 1080s for the skateboarders on the half-pipes!

Once you've realigned your reward structure, it's essential to continue improving your Fluid Form organization. That never-ending process is described in the next chapter.

Step 8: Keep on Ratcheting Upward!

Configuring the Fluid Form Dashboard

The Comanche believed in his magic—though he believed the world was run by magic—only when it worked for him. Once such men had found their medicine they faced the future unafraid. This religion had no ethic, or concept of moral elevation, or notion of reward and punishment.[24]

As Fleetwood Mac sang, "Don't stop thinking about tomorrow!" Once you've completed the initial installation of Fluid Form, you become a little like the painters on the Golden Gate Bridge—as soon as you finish, you start all over again. It's about constantly reviewing and ratcheting upwards. Where else can you create improvement? What other processes can you review? What else can be linked? What other synergies can you find? What work can be eliminated? How else can you tie things together around the actual work instead of the org chart?

How can you continually work on homeroom robustness? How do you manage people in and out of teams? How do you bring more focus and cohesion to the process? In terms of assessing and weaving: are the right people involved making the linkages? How can you make that process more robust, to further flatten the organization? Can you find new, creative ways to make people more rewarded? Can you create opportunities to use your employees' talents and impact on the overall success of the enterprise? How

---

24 Fehrenbach, *Comanches*, 48.

do you maximize the synergy between the success of the individual employees and the enterprises' success?

As noted before, typical organizations follow the classic pyramid organizational chart—with ever-increasing boxes as you move downward until you arrive at the box containing "your job." That is the static concept of an organization. You look at the chart and jobs change at some point in time but not continuously. Fluid Form, on the other hand, is dynamic and is always changing because people are moving in and out of projects and processes. The organization becomes a living entity.

In order to maintain a dynamic environment and really make it work, Fluid Form must be monitored, coordinated, and powered. In a sense, it must have power applied to it at all times—monitoring, and coordinating all the components as they move over time; or as there are adjustments being made; or as there are changes in the business situation. In Fluid Form, you need sufficient infrastructure and power to keep the lights on. Since it is in motion, Fluid Form needs this kind of energy and attention in order to develop. Without adequate power, your organization will revert or retrench to the traditional bureaucratic system. Think of computer memory, or DRAM. It works when the computer is on—when the power is applied. But if you remove the power supply, the memory is gone.

Now think of airplanes and flight controllers. Planes fly, they move, they are dynamic. But a flight controller is monitoring and coordinating all movement. The controller watches multiple planes from an air tower. This way, he or she is able to make adjustments, decisions, and changes. It needs to be the same in your Fluid Form organization. You can't just sit there, because it is dynamic.

Like airplanes, Fluid Form teams also are dynamic—moving in and out. Teams and people come on board and networks change. During these movements, it is important to monitor and assess the following:

• What has changed recently?

- What is in the process of change?
- What needs to change now, or what do you think will need to change down the road?

Through monitoring, you understand what is happening and forecast what is going to happen, so that you can be prepared to respond to it.

Fluid Form Teams are like roving bands of Comanche moving to their attack. They are very focused on a specific goal or task. But after the job is completed, the group disbands and another war party forms. A new chief summons leaders who pull a different mix of people, and they go off on a different project. As the mix of people and the focus changes, you need to watch a team's movements to make sure they fit within a Fluid Form model. Coordinating the ins and outs of people in various projects and networks is critical in making it work. It's a different kind of coordination than we are accustomed to thinking of, and in many ways, it's more active than the coordination required in today's static organization. Fluid Form must be coordinated, powered, and managed.

System Failure

How could a system fail? There are five reasons systems might fail.

1. Lack of monitoring
2. Lack of response
3. Lack of sufficient engineering—to sustain or retain the appropriate degree of robust, Fluid Form infrastructure.
4. Lack of forecasting of future states and scenarios

This is, in part, related to a lack of forward planning or thinking ahead. If you're successful, you're not just looking at what's happening—you're thinking about what needs to happen. Whether situations are short-term or long-term, be prepared to make adjustments.

5.   Lack of attention to interdependent processes and projects

Pay attention to interactive relationships. Look to align them, realign them, and make sure they're in sync to prevent system errors. You can respond, but you have to look at the relationships and observe how they change. If one process or project starts to head in another direction, it may affect two or three others, and you will have to make changes there, too.

Again, we're not taking an organization from Point A to Point B. We're always looking for something new, always ratcheting to greater Fluid Form. The real move is from an org chart to a shifting *configuration* of your assets—your people. The dashboard for that configuration measures performance goals, gaps, list of projects and processes, status, and forecasts. We're looking for synergies and ties across projects—these are all part of the configuration. People are no longer in individual departments or boxes on org charts; instead, they appear in different roles in that ever-shifting configuration of your assets. The configuration is a snapshot of a point in time, not a static chart. Things change: processes begin, end, or are modified. People move, networks change, and the mix of stakeholders changes. The configuration on September 1 won't be the same as the configuration on October 1.

That's Fluid Form. Change is now built into the concept of the organization. Robustness makes it work. If it's robust, you can be flexible and fluid, to meet changing opportunities and situations. You'll have the right people doing the right things at the right time.

So it's time to take another look at all eight steps in the process and begin to view these as the major components of Fluid Form organization. Where are you now on each of these? What needs attention? What needs to be adjusted down the road? What benchmarks are you setting for the future?

Configuring the Fluid Form Dashboard

Step 1: Where Are You Now?
Assess Your "As-Is": Performance Gaps

Have we narrowed the gap? Is our focus right? Do we need to shift direction?

Step 2: Assess Your Cultural Support for Membership Fluidity

Are we moving the culture in the right direction? Where do we need to put our effort next?

Step 3: Assess Your "As-Is": Project/Processes & Functional Initiatives

Are we moving away from functional silos and building process synergy? Where should we focus next?

Step 4: Reduce Your Boundaries

Have we broken down barriers and made it easier to move resources to support the work that needs to get done now? What are the obvious boundaries that need to be opened next?

Step 5: Create the Virtual Homeroom
Developing Robust Fluid Form Teams

Are we building sufficient infrastructure in our teams so they really feel they are a team that is getting the job done? Is the problem-solving technology available for our teams to feel as if they are working in the same room?

Step 6: Assess Coordination Requirements & Weave Networks

Have we built robust networks with the right stakeholders that are providing guidance to teams? Have we actively reduced the number of managers and levels as networks fill the role?

Step 7: Evaluate Reward and Progression Systems

Are we shifting the reward system from moving up the hierarchy to taking on broader challenges within teams and networks? What next steps do we need to take?

Step 8: Keep On Ratcheting Upward!
Configuring the Fluid Form Dashboard

Have we changed our perspective of organization from a static chart to a dynamic array of teams and networks? Are we monitoring and actively coordinating the system components? Are we looking to the future, to the next level of Fluid Form?

Embracing Fluid Form

Many approaches to changing organizations for improved effectiveness have been heralded as the guiding light or derided as the flavor of the month. Some ideas stick and make a difference. Some receive attention and time, but cost much more than they produce of value. Any organization change has inertia and barriers that try to pull it back to the way things were. While moving to Fluid Form confronts the same obstacles as any change, there is an inherent advantage in the build sequence that presents a lower profile and seems less like a looming change effort. Because the basic element of Fluid Form is building robust project teams, for the people on these teams, providing powerful tools and the support systems to make them work does not feel like a change. It just feels like the natural process of improving how things work.

There are four guidelines that can support implementation without raising the "flag of change" and the resistance that usually goes with it. These may become trapdoors where an organization can fall into the pits that generate resistance and devour time money and energy. To avoid these pitfalls, the trapdoors that reduce the likelihood of successful change must be reviewed in the context of building a Fluid Form organization.

Transferability

Change efforts often are viewed as an adjunct activity to the real business at hand. As such, they carry a second-class status that translates into lack of interest or action, because the real work seems more pressing and important. This phenomenon is more likely to occur when the work is viewed as not tied to, or distantly related to, the organization's fundamental goals and initiatives. If it is clear that leaning the organization is essential to support projects and processes directly targeted to improve the company's performance, then the change effort is seen as turbo-charging the work that needs to get done, as opposed to taking precious time away from that very work. Only by transferring new systems into the existing business practices as quickly as possible will they be viewed and assimilated as the practices in use.

Cycle Time

The time it takes to effect organization change is a balancing act between forcing in a new system versus dragging a process on so long it becomes another bureaucratic layer of work instead of a process to reduce bureaucracy. It would be smarter to take the amount of leanness the organization will give in a relatively short period rather than go for a larger change over an extended period of time. This approach fits the philosophy of Fluid Form evolution, which is to continually build more robust teams while periodically moving the larger organization system to greater leanness. This builds change capability into the very core concept of the organization, with the expectation that fluidity and performance go hand-in-hand.

Scope

Some organizations use different methodologies or standards for management than for non-management employees, and a separate—or no—methodology for executives. One of the greatest failings of implementing the socio-technical systems developed in the seventies was focusing the new system almost exclusively on the non-management sector. While first-level supervision was eliminated in many cases, the rest of the management system retained much the same form and practices as it had previously. The scope of change needs to encompass the entire organization. The optimum level of lean cannot be achieved if several high levels of management want to retain their traditional way of doing business, comfortable with the hierarchal and functional differentiation to which they are accustomed.

Nonetheless, when the time seems right to redesign the larger superstructure— a shift from hierarchy to networks—to support a project/process based organization, the traditional barriers to change will begin to emerge. If project teams have been successful, the need to lean out the superstructure might be so obvious that resistance is decreased. Ultimately, Fluid Form becomes synonymous with change, as projects start, stop, and reformulate to meet the needs at hand. This becomes how work is done, and no longer a "change effort."

If Fluid Form teams are robust and networks are woven to support and guide them, then the extent of the hierarchal system will be seen as unnecessary. Removing pieces of the hierarchy over time will not encounter the usual resistance, because a better system is already in place.

Energy

Once a new system has been implemented, it should be self-sustaining. You shouldn't need to keep pumping energy into change efforts to resuscitate or improve them. If you constantly need to involve executives to support new systems, or constantly need to involve more people or money, then the effort has not taken hold and is not yet part of the way work gets done. The solutions should work, and teams across the organization should soon feel that this is the way to get things done, a natural evolution to a better way. Making project teams more robust and supporting them should be recognized as making it easier to participate effectively on these teams, and the teams should see results faster and with less effort. Leaning the organization should be experienced just as the name implies—it should feel leaner, more efficient, and less bureaucratic, with fewer obstacles and time-consuming sign-offs on the path to achieving results. The energy level in the organization should be higher than in the past, as success breeds enthusiasm.

The elements of building robust Fluid Form infrastructure are far more thorough and complex than typically envisioned. Nonetheless, if the effectiveness that many organizations have come to believe can be derived from project and process teams, then the investment in this comprehensive infrastructure is small compared to the investment of the resources and time assigned to them. Without sufficient infrastructure the full benefit of horizontal organization remains unrealized. With it, outstanding project performance becomes the norm and Fluid Form capability is happily achieved.

So don't stop thinking about tomorrow. Keep on finding ways to increase the fluidity of the form of your organization, so you can continue to become flatter, faster, a better place to work, and—at the end of the day—vastly more profitable.

Afterword

Beyond the Business World

Fluid Form can work in areas beyond the business world. It can be useful in nonprofits, and even can be used to solve some of the most intractable social problems we face. Many of the major global issues, such as the environment, health care, hunger, and education, seem incapable of resolution today. It seems as though our current efforts are more like putting our "fingers in the dike"—only to produce results that fail to achieve critical mass, and that fail to gather sufficient momentum and direction to indicate that success is possible and visible over some meaningful time frame.

Is it possible that the most important and difficult of these issues on which we have been hard-pressed to make headway might be more readily resolved in a world where Fluid Form organizations are prevalent? Effective collaboration and creative solutions that are closeted by hierarchal controls become realizable in a Fluid Form world, where business-to-business and business-to-government can operate in a truly more open environment.

For those who know me, it's no secret that I am frustrated with the politics of change. The possibility for collaboration seems more daunting as national competition for resources and religious self-absorption build barriers to the superordinate requirements for planetary survival. Government initiatives fall short, do not develop momentum, and show little creativity or experimentation. Yet, most of us look to, and rely on, initiatives developed politically and executed by bureaucracies to resolve the big issues.

There is a smaller group who believe that real movement toward results lies within the individual. When enough people begin to center their own thoughts and efforts, through meditation or the discipline of personal change, large-scale change is achievable.

There may not be enough horsepower behind either of these approaches when it comes to solving the major planetary issues. It is through organizations that the rules of engagement for business and for nations are determined. The way that we organize shapes the way organizations interact. Considering that we rule today's world via organization, it is not unreasonable to believe that a different organizational form might also produce much of the horsepower required to affect global issues.

Fluid Form to Fluid Form creates a different system for problem-solving, decision-making, resolution, and action supported across businesses, governments and nations.

The major issues today are not unrelated. It is likely that successful initiatives in the environment, health care, hunger, and education will have effects on the other issues. In a Fluid Form environment, networks that find and create solutions in one venue are likely to connect and discover that similar approaches work in another context.

In effecting organizational change, the practitioner's rule of thumb has been that if 15 to 20 percent of the workforce learns a better way of solving problems, the culture of the larger organization will shift and begin to work in that way as well. In other words, changing how things get done does not require *everyone* to see and do things differently. Critical mass is much less than most people expected would be needed.

No Child Left Behind ... Without A Computer

The federal No Child Left Behind Law aimed at raising the nation's educational performance, especially for the basics, has been controversial from state to state and from teachers to students and their parents. This pressure for performance measured by standardized tests intersects the belief that if each child had a computer, they would be more successful at school. The result is that the big computer and software companies eagerly market school systems statewide or locally to be the technology of choice. The education administrations barter with these companies, state funding agencies and foundations for the money and pricing deals to make this happen.

What gets lost in all this is the implementation plan for how computers will be used to teach and how teachers will be trained to use them. What also gets lost is the involvement of teachers, parents and even students to ensure that there is a true educational benefit. So, as the big parties cut the deals, the often reluctant and angry teachers are left with the hardware and software and little motivation or knowledge about how to effectively make use of them. Once again, there is room for a Fluid Form approach that puts the main constituencies together to build a program that has real value for the kids.

On the broader and even more important issue of education in general, I wonder why we haven't tried more out-of-the-box approaches. Suppose there was a project that was built on helping kids find out what there talents and interests were, very early in life. For any specific line of interest, a child might be immersed in the many aspects of the field that turned it into a career. Perhaps there would be no degree, and no ties to the current system of high schools and college. Doing so would require organizations that needed individuals with these talents to fund and be part of the educational process, and to have employment available—at least initially—for the participants when they were ready, not when they got their degree.

Making this happen would require an inter-organizational network robust enough to be successful alongside the traditional system. Whatever succeeded could, in time, be mainstreamed.

Reformulating Health Care

One of the many healthcare issues that incite frustration and even anger centers on new drug introductions, especially for insidious diseases like cancer. The FDA is accused either of waiting too long to release new, life-saving possibilities, or of caving in too soon to drug companies eager for profits from potentially gangbuster drugs. Meanwhile, sick and dying individuals and their families are eager to try promising new drugs. They trust neither the FDA nor the major drug companies. In the middle, the HMOs and managed care providers flinch at the high cost of new releases and normally promote older drug solutions, especially when costs are much lower.

Today, these organizations work independently and often at cross-purposes. What if, on just this one type of cancer, there was a project to come up with a plan closer to the win-win that often emerges from those GE Work-Outs? If that worked better than the system is working today, wouldn't that likely spawn other, similar projects for other specific diseases? The process of doing this would surely change to make it continuously more effective. In time, there might exist more broadly accepted inter-organizational networks to move new drugs into the marketplace—an array of projects that operates across organizational boundaries. What prevents this from happening is likely the tradition of organizational isolation that still dominates.

We govern the planet today with verticals facing off with other verticals. Do you really think that even one world government in vertical form could successfully solve the big issues? Hierarchies limit our ability to forge trans-national agreements. Fluid Form organizations might break the gridlock. Even a small percentage of them be would enough to establish a beachhead. These horizontally-woven networks could escape the usual win/lose dynamics, which typify the way in which the verticals have put solution-finding into to the cryogenic deep freeze. This would be a more substantial approach to resolving global warming, for example, than that being undertaken by the present international consortiums.

Despite all that has been achieved and learned about organizing around processes, building teams, and measuring results—both in the human and technical dimensions—it's harder than anyone thought to build horizontal success inside a vertical system. The inertia of tradition, of how organizations have been working, is ingrained into us all.

When will you know if Fluid Form is beginning to take hold? When the horizontals (the project teams) have sufficient resources and support, when they are not driven to extinction or uselessness by the hierarchy, when they are seen as where the real work gets done, and when their members get continuously more exciting and challenging projects. When this happens, you will know.

Fluid Form is a different approach to organizing. It is the future. And now, it is in your hands.

FLUID FORM ASSESSMENT

1	2	3	4	5
Not very good	Poor	Fair	Good	Very Good

Fluid Form Assessment

(1) Performing on important measures of success?	1 2 3 4 5
(2) Supporting a collaborative culture?	1 2 3 4 5
(3) Linking processes and functional initiatives?	1 2 3 4 5
(4) Removing boundaries between functions?	1 2 3 4 5
(5) Constructing robust cross-functional teams?	1 2 3 4 5
(6) Getting fewer managers to cover more process and functional areas?	1 2 3 4 5
(7) Shifting success from moving up the ladder to taking challenging roles?	1 2 3 4 5
(8) Monitoring and actively coordinating the Fluid Form Dashboard?	1 2 3 4 5

The aim of the *Fluid Form Assessment* is to provoke thought about where the organization stands on the development of Fluid Form capability.

Gap analysis: Plot your organization's X and Y ratings for each item on the survey.

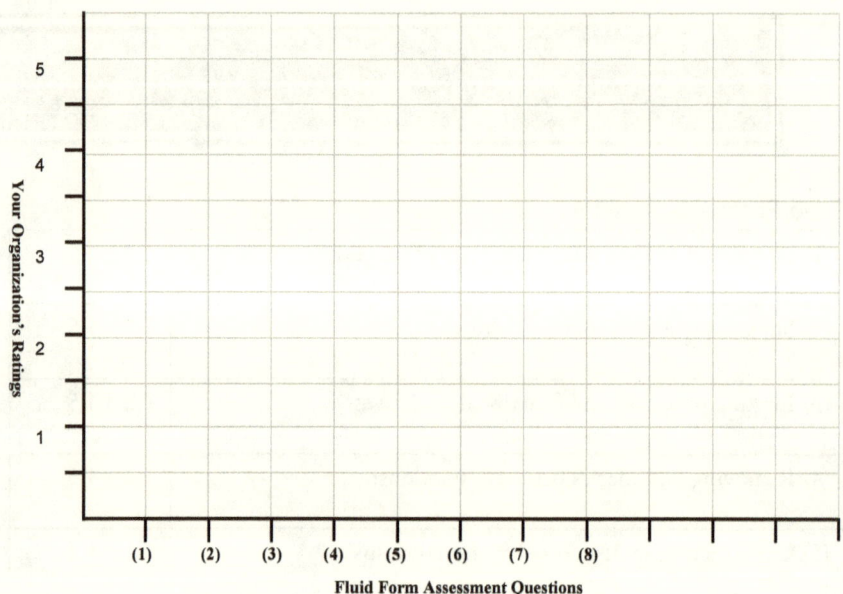

Summary

Guidelines for the 8 Steps

Step 1: Where Are You Now?
Assess Your "As-Is": Performance Gaps

Where do you currently stand on your most important measures of success? Where is your organization operating below standard? What areas need to be "ratcheted up"?

Consider how you stack up in areas like these:

- Responding to customers/stakeholders
- Meeting objectives
- Developing focused, measurable initiatives
- Managing key business processes across functions
- Balancing people/skill requirements within budget limitations
- Aligning performance assessment with company goals
- Developing a collaborative culture aimed at improvement

Step 2: Assess Your Cultural Support for Membership Fluidity

Where is your organization currently in terms of cultural support for fluidity—the approach to leadership, decision-making, how people will work together, and what's expected of individuals and teams?

- Employee Knowledge: What level of knowledge are employees expected to have about the organization's objectives in relationship to their job?

- On-the-Job Learning: To what degree are employees expected to learn on the job, or to expand their skills to other job areas?

- Collaboration: What is the expected balance between independent work and collaborative work within or across teams?

- Process Orientation: To what extent is the organization focused on work processes and their improvement, rather than compartmentalized by job, department, and/or function?

- Job Flexibility: How will the organization allow for the design or redesign of jobs versus strictly adhering to strict job descriptions? How easily can employees work outside of the confines of their job descriptions?

- Individual Input: How much are people involved in providing input to their operational area? Do they have the freedom to make independent decisions for the benefit of the business?

- Voice in Change: How much say do people have in designing the change(s) and in being a part of the transition to an improved organization?

You also want to ask yourself the following key questions:

- How could this type of cultural change move forward?
- How big a cultural shift will you need to make?
- Where do anticipate resistance, and what is your plan to overcome it?

Envision cultural support of membership fluidity as a checklist of what needs to happen in order to develop Fluid Form.

Step 3: Assess Your "As-Is":
Project/Processes & Functional Initiatives

Most organizations today have a mix of functional and process initiatives. To get an idea of how you're doing at what you do, first ask: what exactly is it that you do? Rethinking your organization through Fluid Form eyes, you will first need to take an inventory and list key Initiatives, Processes, Projects, Activities (Councils, Committees, etc.). Simply stated, what works together and what doesn't?

Here are the questions to ask:

- What do you have in place already in terms of process, projects and activities?
- Which of those are major processes and which of those are working well and already are oriented correctly?
- Which of those have good coordination and have the right depth of experience and people on them?
- And how well are they working with their stakeholders and other important people to get the job done?

Many organizations begin to take inventory, but they fail to see the entire scope of their performance. They tend to focus on functional performance rather than linking related functional and process activities and objectives.

Identify and assess your functional initiatives:

- Are they too specialized?
- Are they too centralized?
- Are some functions undermining processes?

- Is there adequate coordination of activities across functions?

- Are the right people involved? Should people in other functions be involved?

- Are the right stakeholders involved for quick decision-making and support?

- Should your functional initiatives be more process-oriented?

What we're really asking are these crucial questions: How well are your processes and functional initiatives linked? How thick and insular are the functional silos?

Next, with the list, describe the links of any related components to determine:

- Level of interdependence
- Coordination required
- Potential synergy or conflict

You will probably find that many of the functional initiatives need to become more process-oriented. It doesn't mean that they all have to be set up to be cross-functional, but should they be more inclusive? In order to really be effective, you will need to get a handle on all of the work and determine the extent of process development that makes the most sense in achieving your objectives.

Step 4: Reduce Your Boundaries

Reduce boundaries to reduce complexity—that's the goal. Where possible, reduce the number of departments, functions, processes, or processes-and-initiatives combined to:

- Reduce complexity
- Link related work
- Determine the level of work that must be managed locally
- Determine the type and level of work that can be managed centrally
- Determine Process/Project Teams for cross-functional construction

Key questions to consider:

- How can you reframe "organizational structure" as an array of project teams with changing membership based on area of focus?
- Where can you reduce or remove functional groupings?
- Where does it really make sense to draw a boundary?

Step 5: Create the Virtual Homeroom

Developing Robust Fluid Form Teams

Five Requirements for Constructing Robust Fluid Form Teams:

- Role and Membership Fluidity
- Team Self-Sustainability
- Integrated Problem Solving and Action Planning Tools
- Open Boundaries
- Comprehensive Scorecards or Dashboards

Role and Membership Fluidity

When defining individual roles for Fluid Form teams, the standard set of variables includes:

- Expertise offered
- Specific contribution expected
- Level of involvement (core, support, review)
- Time commitment

Membership fluidity means the ability to accommodate an array of changes in the composition and roles of project participants. The ability of a team to accommodate each of these determines what might be called a fluidity index:

- "On-boarding" new participants and getting them up to speed
- Removing participants for good cause, without prejudice

- Expanding an existing role because of interest or capability
- Reducing the task load because of interest or to balance other assignments
- Changing the composition of the role or exchanging roles
- Adding elements of team coordination or leadership

Team Self-Sustainability

The set of skills required include the ability to:

- Define key issues
- Prioritize key issues
- Develop solutions
- Agree upon critical actions
- Determine responsibility for assignments and action plans
- Accept accountability for individual assignments
- Rigorously monitor all team project variables
- Maintain critical interface relationships
- Build confidence
- Build energy and momentum

Integrated Problem-Solving and Action-Planning Tools

The homeroom information system must contain a minimum standard set of integrated tools that allow for reasonable customization to the situation at hand just as one would expect to be able to do when everyone is in one room, to support the following activities:

- Surveys—rating scales, multiple choice, open-ended
- Brainstorming—lists, categorized lists, force field analysis

- Decision-Making—ranking against one or more criteria, checklists

- Action-Planning—Responsibilities, deadlines, resources needed

- Progress and Scorecards—Task status, forecasting, results tracking

Open Boundaries

Opening and managing boundaries by connecting and checking in with other, related projects increases support for success. Fluid form teams build into the coordination and leadership tasks just this sort of active communication, to maintain links to:

- Sponsors and key executives
- Related initiatives and projects

Comprehensive Scorecards or Dashboards

An active scorecard provides a real-time feedback loop to insure that the right work is getting done and that the ball isn't being dropped on one part of the project when it's supposed to connect to another element operating in parallel. Key elements to consider:

- Are metrics defined and understood by team members?
- Are the tools available to analyze the data, and construct an appropriately sensitive monitoring system?
- Is there real time information about progress?
- Are connections to related projects and to key organization initiatives visible?

Step 6: Assess Coordination Requirements & Weave Networks

Take a look at management to determine how much and what type of coordination/leadership is required for each project/process team relative to:

- Setting overall direction and developing strategy
- Deploying projects, initiatives, processes, and the teams associated with them
- Allocating human and financial capital to specific parts of the organization
- Motivating, harnessing, and focusing energy and enthusiasm
- Evaluating individual performance and providing feedback for improvement
- Determining where an individual stands relative to meritorious compensation

Instead of appointing leaders, establish coordination/leadership networks that will supplant unnecessary management and support linked arrays of Fluid Form teams. Who are the stakeholders that should be involved in decision making for each:

- Project/Process?
- Linked Set?

The key questions are:

- Can these specified decision-making networks provide the required coordination and leadership, or is a single "manager in charge" required?

- Can fewer managers cover more process and functional areas, because of greater intra-project capability?

- What is the minimum number of hierarchical levels required to insure coordination, leadership and best decisions?

Step 7: Evaluate Reward and Progression Systems

Key issues to consider:

- Are you rewarding people for participation on multiple projects outside of their functional group?

- Are you making it clear that this work is just as important as what they accomplish within their functional group?

- Are you encouraging your employees to take ownership for new roles and challenges?

- Are you shifting your concept of success from moving up the hierarchy to filling roles and assignments that move the business and the organization ahead?

- Does the appraisal process include the right people from all the relevant projects and networks?

Step 8: Keep on Ratcheting Upward!

Configuring the Fluid Form Dashboard

It's about constantly reviewing and ratcheting upwards. In order to maintain a dynamic environment and really make it work, Fluid Form must be monitored, coordinated, and powered at all times. The real move is from an org chart to a shifting *configuration* of where you are on the 8 Steps today.

Configuring the Fluid Form Dashboard

It is important to monitor and assess the following on all 8 Steps:

- What has changed recently?
- What is in the process of change?
- What needs to change now, or what do you think will need to change down the road?

Step 1: Assess Your "As-Is": Performance Gaps

- Have we narrowed the gap?
- Is our focus right?
- Do we need to shift direction?

Step 2: Assess Your Cultural Support for Membership Fluidity

- Are we moving the culture in the right direction?
- Where do we need to put our effort next?

Step 3: Assess Your Project/Processes & Functional Initiatives

- Are we moving away from functional silos and building process synergy?
- Where should we focus next?

Step 4: Reduce Your Boundaries

- Have we broken down barriers and made it easier to move resources to support the work that needs to get done now?
- What are the obvious boundaries that need to be opened next?

Step 5: Create the Virtual Homeroom

- Are we building sufficient infrastructure in our teams so they really feel they are a team that is getting the job done?
- Is the problem-solving technology available for our teams to feel as if they are working in the same room?

Step 6: Assess Coordination Requirements & Weave Networks

- Have we built robust networks with the right stakeholders that are providing guidance to teams?
- Have we actively reduced the number of managers and levels as networks fill the role?

Step 7: Evaluate Reward and Progression Systems

- Are we shifting the reward system from moving up the hierarchy to taking on broader challenges within teams and networks?
- What next steps do we need to take?

Step 8: Keep on Ratcheting Upward!

- Have we changed our perspective of organization from a static chart to a dynamic array of teams and networks?
- Are we monitoring and actively coordinating the system components of the Fluid Form Dashboard?
- Are we looking to the future, to the next level of Fluid Form?

Works Cited

Bialik, Carl. "Far Removed from Proof of 'Six Degrees' Theory" *Wall Street Journal.* August 6, 2008.

Fehrenbach, T.R., *Comanches: The Destruction of a People.* New York: Knopf, 1974.

Graves, J. Peter. *Success Effectiveness Chart.* California State University, San Bernardino. 1979.

MacIntyre, John. "Corporate America Stuck in Meetings." *San Jose Mercury News.* April 2, 2006.

Maslow, Abraham. *Toward A Psychology of Being.* New York: John Wiley & Sons, 1968.

"The New Organization." *The Economist.* January 21, 2006.

Ritsuko, Ando. *Reuters.* July 8, 2008

Senge, Peter, Scharmer, C. O., Jaworski, J., Flowers, B., *Presence: Human Purpose and the Field of the Future.* Cambridge, MA: Society for Organizational Learning, 2004.

Should we continue the conversation?

Typically I work with Fortune 500 companies to achieve step-function gains in productivity and effectiveness by integrating Fluid Form concepts.

If you are interested in learning more about Fluid Form Organization please visit **www.TheFutureIsFluidForm.com**

I have been developing software to support Fluid Form implementation and am interested in qualified partners to pursue customized applications. For more information visit **www.ChangeCompanion.com**

About the Author

Ord Elliott has four decades of experience as an internal and external management consultant for companies such as Procter and Gamble, General Electric, Allied Signal, Shell Oil, Pacific Gas and Electric, Intel, Philips, Cisco Systems, and numerous Silicon Valley start-ups. Visit him online at **www.TheFutureIsFluidForm.com.**